SUPERHEROES

Illustrated by
Justin Thompson
and
Jael

Kidsbooks®

Copyright © 2007, 2006 Kidsbooks LLC
www.kidsbooks.com

Manufactured in China

0407-3C

Visit us at www.kidsbooks.com®

INTRODUCTION

This book will show you how to draw lots of superheroes.
Some are more difficult than others, but if you follow along, step-by-step, you will soon be able
to draw many different cartoon characters.

SUPPLIES

Soft pencils (#2 or softer)
Soft eraser
Drawing pad

Fine-line markers
Colored pencils
Markers or crayons

Each drawing in this book begins with a line drawing or stick figure.
This establishes the figure's movement. Then different shapes, mainly ovals, are added
over the line figure to round out its basic shapes.

HELPFUL HINTS

1. Take your time with steps 1 and 2. In the first two steps of each drawing, you will create a solid foundation of the figure—much like a builder who must construct a foundation before building the rest of the house. Next comes the fun part—creating a smooth, clean outline of the cartoon character, then adding all the finishing touches, such as details, shading, and color.

Note: Following the first two steps carefully will make the final steps easier.

2. Always keep your pencil lines light and soft. This will make the guidelines easier to erase when you no longer need them.

3. Don't be afraid to erase. It usually takes a lot of sketching and erasing before you will be satisfied with the way your drawing looks. Each image has special character-istics that make it easier or, in some cases, harder to draw. However, it is easier to draw anything if you first break it down into simple shapes.

4. Add details and all the finishing touches only *after* you have blended and refined all the shapes and your drawing is complete.

5. Remember: Practice makes perfect. Don't be discouraged if you don't get the hang of it right away. Just keep drawing, erasing, and redrawing until you do.

HOW TO START

1. Begin by drawing the basic line drawing or stick figure, such as the one in step 1 below, for a general outline of the figure. Usually, it is easier to begin by drawing the largest shape first. Dotted lines show what can be erased as you go along.

2. Sketch the other shapes over the first ones. These are the basic guidelines that create the foundation of your drawing.

Note: Remember to keep your lines lightly drawn, erasing any guidelines you no longer need as you go along.

3. Carefully combine and blend all the lines and shapes to create the final outline, so that the figure has a smooth, flowing look. Then start adding the details that make this character unique.

4. Continue to refine your drawing as you darken the hair and other areas, and add final details and finishing touches. When your figure is complete, color it with your favorite colors or, for a more dramatic effect, outline it with a thick black marker.

Use your imagination and feel free to create details other than the ones shown. You may even want to add backgrounds to enhance your drawings. When you have drawn some or all of the awesome animated characters in this book and are comfortable with your drawing technique, start creating your own.

Most of all, HAVE FUN!

Foreshortening

Many cartoon figures are shown in dramatic poses that include *foreshortening*. To understand this better, stand in front of a mirror and point to yourself with one arm. See how short your arm appears? Then hold your other arm straight out to your side. Now you can see your arm's normal length. An artist learns to draw things as the eye sees them, not as they really are. This gives the figure a realistic, three-dimensional appearance.

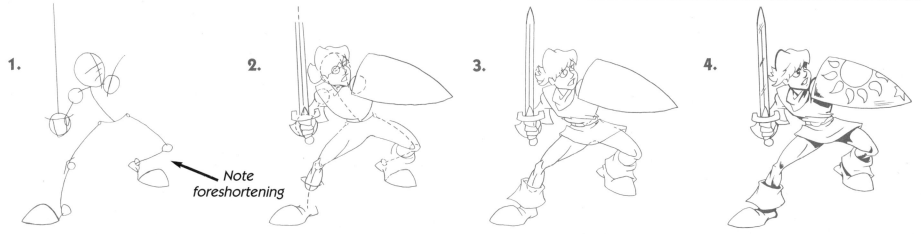

1.

Note foreshortening

2.

3.

4.

Z. Charger

1. Begin by lightly sketching simple guideline shapes, as shown—ovals, curved lines, squares, and a triangle.

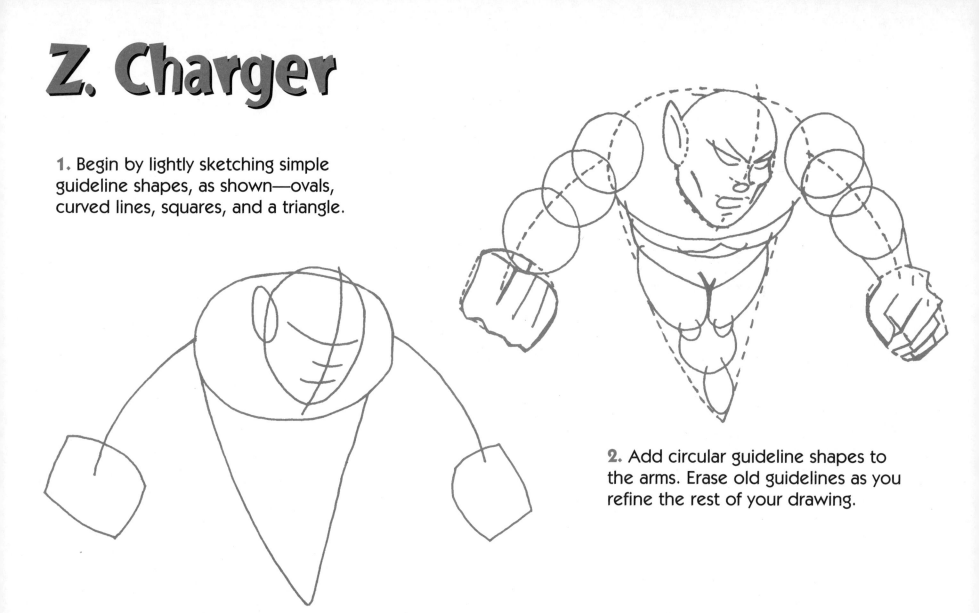

2. Add circular guideline shapes to the arms. Erase old guidelines as you refine the rest of your drawing.

Tip: The way the lower body of this character is drawn is an example of foreshortening.

3. Further define the arms, hands, and face. Add hair to this high-flying character's head, then begin drawing the charger stripes on his outfit.

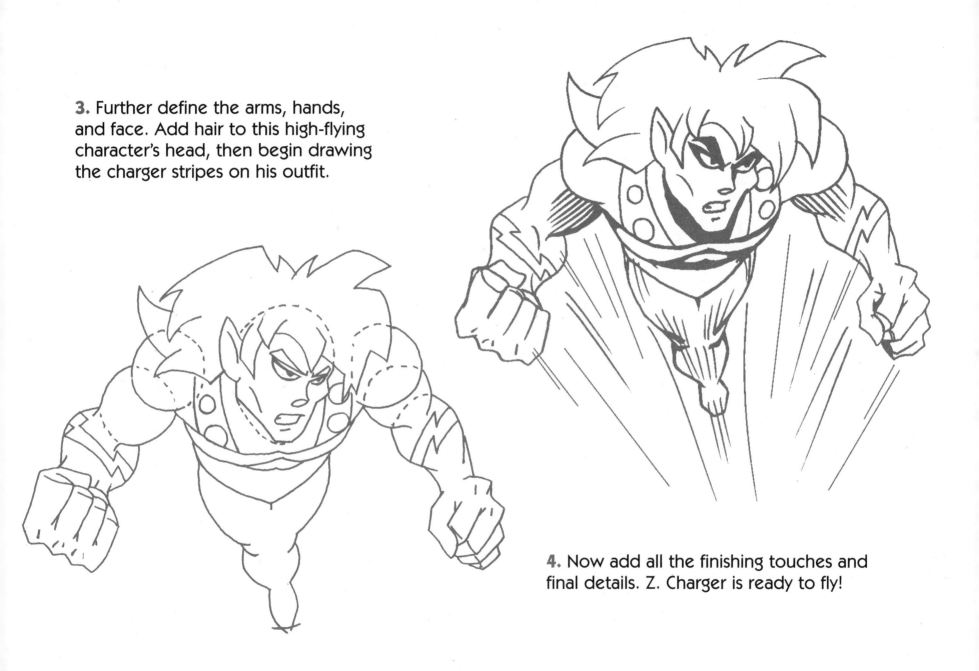

4. Now add all the finishing touches and final details. Z. Charger is ready to fly!

She-La Z

2. Create two bladelike shapes for the hair. Draw large ovals to define the arms, legs, and feet. Refine the waist and upper body. Then begin adding facial features.

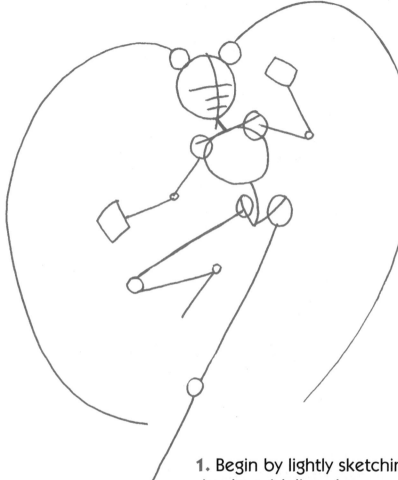

1. Begin by lightly sketching simple guideline shapes—circles, ovals, squares, and curved lines.

Tip: Always keep your pencil lines light and soft when drawing these first steps, so your guidelines will be easier to erase later.

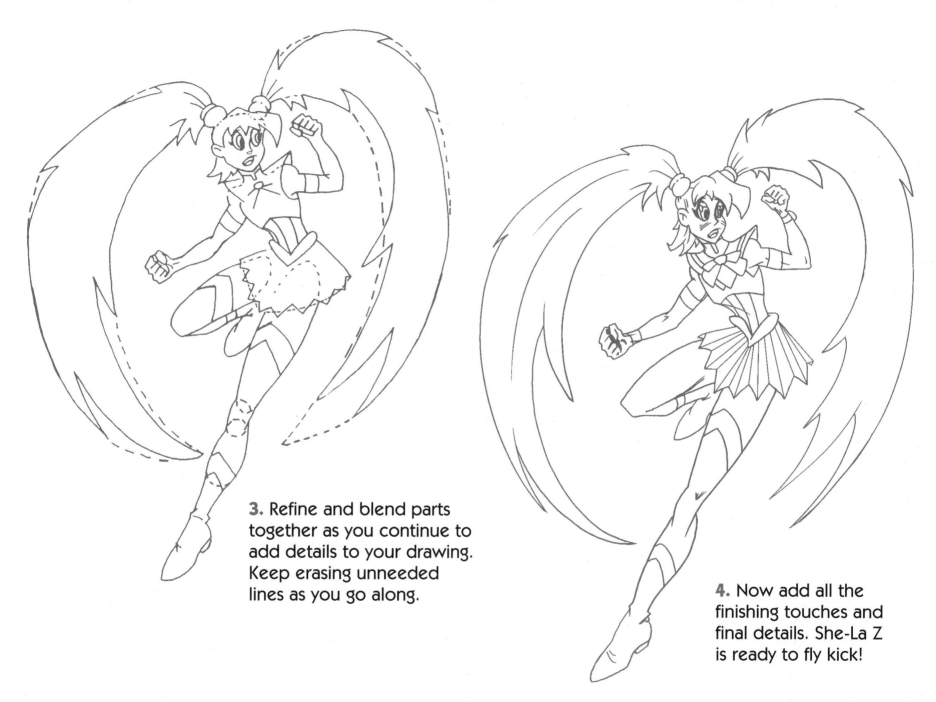

3. Refine and blend parts together as you continue to add details to your drawing. Keep erasing unneeded lines as you go along.

4. Now add all the finishing touches and final details. She-La Z is ready to fly kick!

Blade Rider

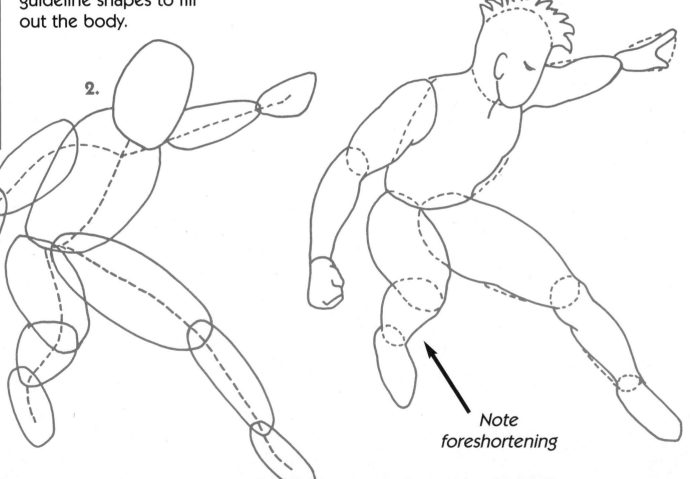

1. & 2. Starting with the head, draw the simple stick figure (gesture lines). Then add the various ovals and other guideline shapes to fill out the body.

3. Start defining and shaping the muscles within the oval guidelines, erasing your gesture lines as you go along. Then begin outlining this superhero's hair, hands, and face. Make sure that you are satisfied with the way your drawing looks before going on to the next step.

Use foreshortening when any part of the body points away from or toward you, the viewer. This will give your figure a dramatic, 3-D look.

Tip: Focus on one part of the body at a time, sketching and erasing until you are satisfied.

Note foreshortening

5. Now add all the final details and finishing touches, and Blade Rider will be ready for action!

4. Complete the facial features and sharply define Blade Rider's arms, legs, and chest muscles. Then begin adding clothes and other details.

Melinda Moderna

1. Draw a large oval shape that is not complete. Then add a smaller, complete oval with guidelines for the facial features. Add the lines for her neck.

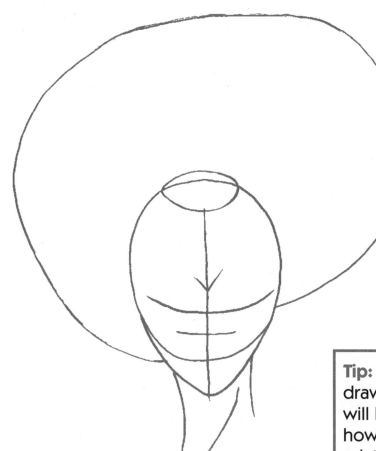

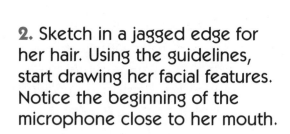

Tip: Studying the step 4 drawing before you begin will help you understand how the basic shapes relate to each other.

2. Sketch in a jagged edge for her hair. Using the guidelines, start drawing her facial features. Notice the beginning of the microphone close to her mouth.

3. Sketch a number 7 onto her forehead and keep refining her facial features and microphone. Draw in her necklace.

4. Shade in the areas shown, and finish the final details. Now Melinda Moderna is ready to rock her world.

It-Zak Cloud Maker

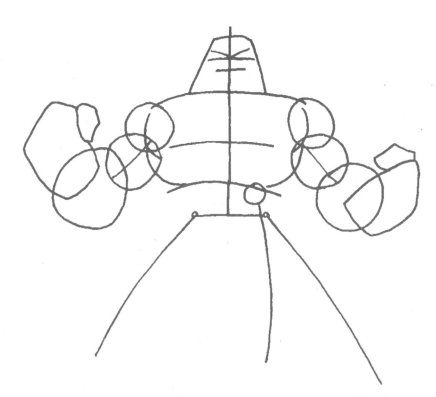

1. Start by drawing a stick figure. Add a large oval shape for his chest and smaller ovals for his arms. Add a rectangular shape for his head. Don't forget the guidelines for his face.

2. Begin designing his facial features, legs, and fists. Add hair and the cloud at his feet. Sketch in his belt, then start drawing the lines for his robe.

3. Erase all the dotted lines from steps 1 and 2. Create a smooth outline for It-Zak Cloud Maker's body. Continue to design his facial features, fists, and robe.

Tip: Practice makes perfect. Don't be discouraged if you don't get the hang of it right away. Just keep drawing and erasing until you do.

4. Erase all guidelines you no longer need. Then add the finishing touches, darkening the areas shown.

Hanna Hardhit

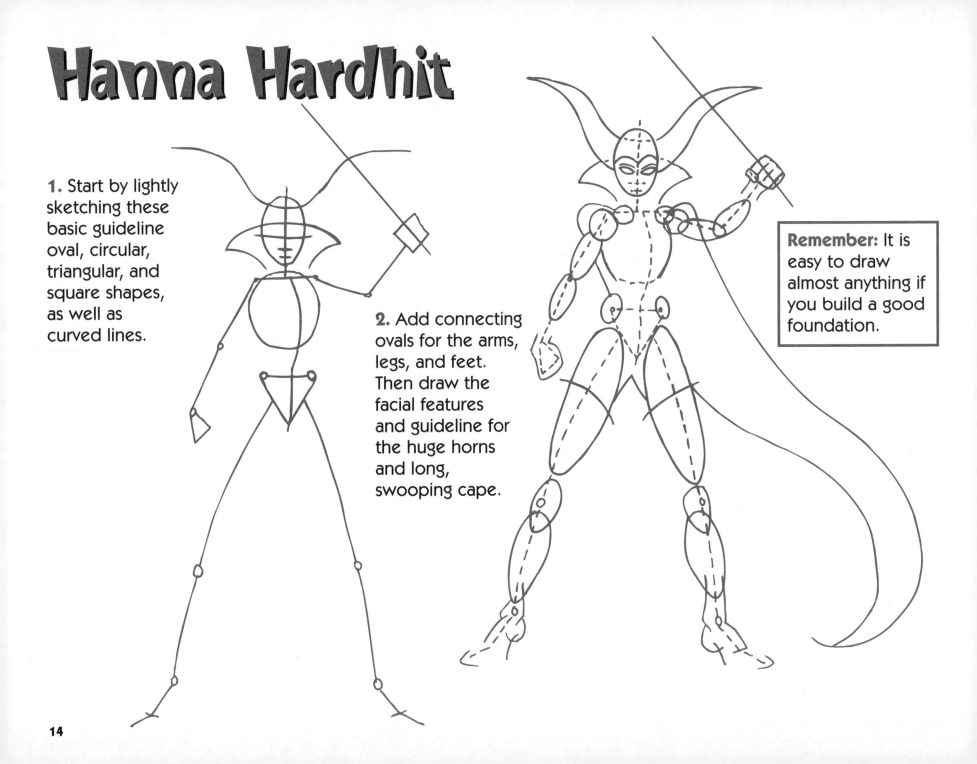

1. Start by lightly sketching these basic guideline oval, circular, triangular, and square shapes, as well as curved lines.

2. Add connecting ovals for the arms, legs, and feet. Then draw the facial features and guideline for the huge horns and long, swooping cape.

Remember: It is easy to draw almost anything if you build a good foundation.

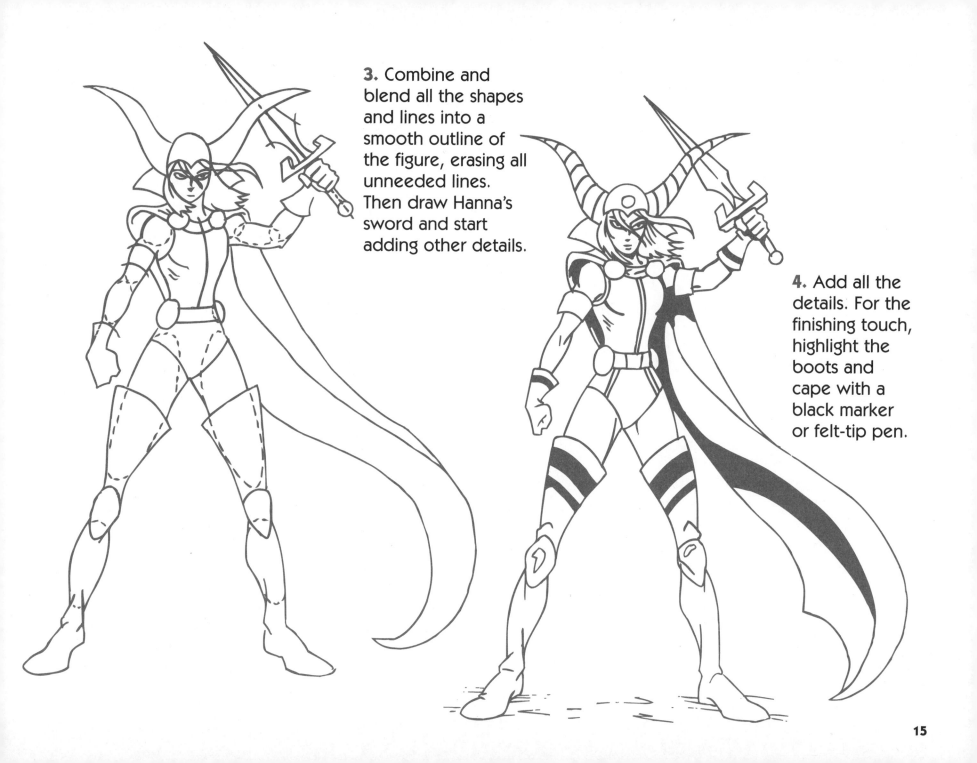

3. Combine and blend all the shapes and lines into a smooth outline of the figure, erasing all unneeded lines. Then draw Hanna's sword and start adding other details.

4. Add all the details. For the finishing touch, highlight the boots and cape with a black marker or felt-tip pen.

15

Kristal Ball

Tip: No one gets it right the first time! Erasing and redrawing are important parts of the process.

1. To draw this character in profile, start with an oval for the head, then add the curved lines for the hair. Next, draw the crossed lines. (They will guide you in creating the nose, lips, and chin in step 2.) Add a small oval for the ear and a *V* shape for the eye.

2. Now create the nose, lips, and chin. Erase guidelines as you go.

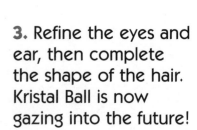

3. Refine the eyes and ear, then complete the shape of the hair. Kristal Ball is now gazing into the future!

The Vaporizer

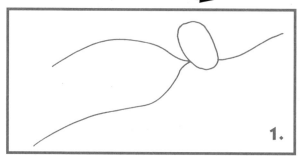

1.

1. & 2. Draw the basic stick figure, then all the overlapping oval body-shape guidelines.

Tip: Make sure that you have built a solid foundation with the first two steps before continuing.

3. Sketch the body parts within the oval guidelines. Begin forming the Vaporizer's hands and facial features (note how his chin juts out), erasing guidelines as you go along.

4. Blend the arm, shoulder, and chest muscles into a smooth upper-body shape. Finish the facial features and add the vaporizing lines coming out of his eye. Extend the flowing body and right-hand lines, then add the final details.

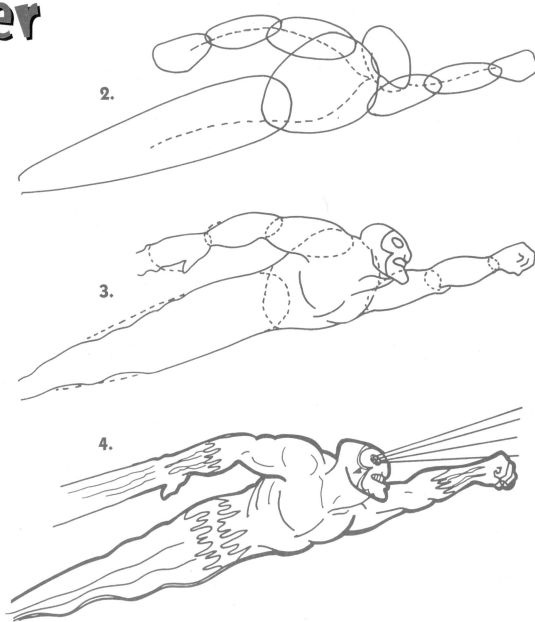

2.

3.

4.

Kit the Courageous

1.

Remember: Erase the stick figure and the other guidelines when they are no longer needed.

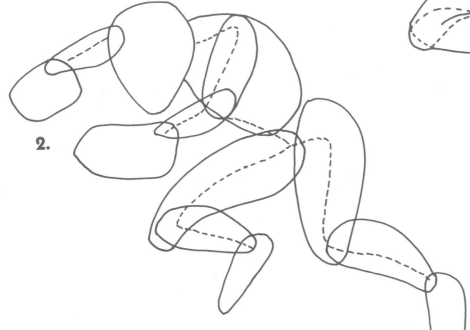

1. & 2. After creating the basic stick figure, add the guideline body shapes. Note that the right arm looks short because part of it is hidden behind the head. To help figure out how to draw this, stand in front of a mirror and try this pose.

2.

3. Combine the shapes with smoothly drawn lines. Define the hands and facial features and add guidelines for Kit's hair and skirt.

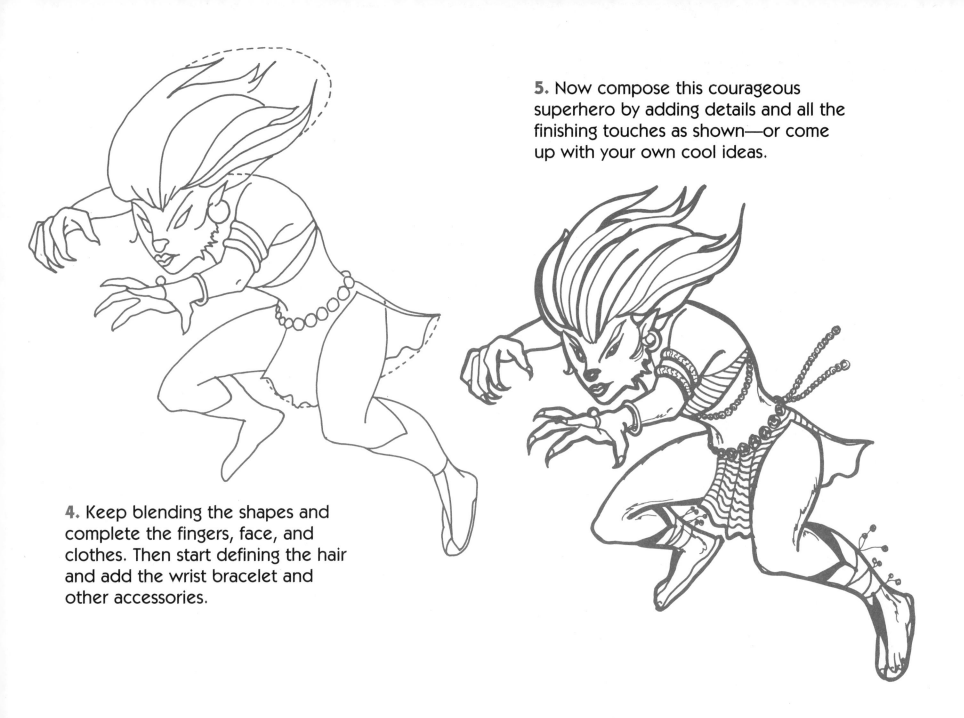

5. Now compose this courageous superhero by adding details and all the finishing touches as shown—or come up with your own cool ideas.

4. Keep blending the shapes and complete the fingers, face, and clothes. Then start defining the hair and add the wrist bracelet and other accessories.

Eric Staffman

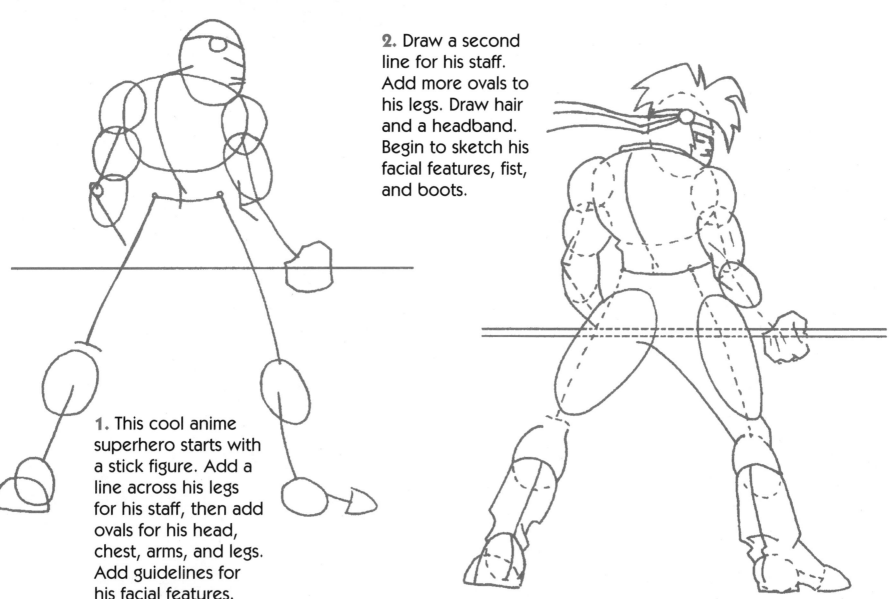

2. Draw a second line for his staff. Add more ovals to his legs. Draw hair and a headband. Begin to sketch his facial features, fist, and boots.

1. This cool anime superhero starts with a stick figure. Add a line across his legs for his staff, then add ovals for his head, chest, arms, and legs. Add guidelines for his facial features.

3. Create a smooth outline, erasing all the dotted lines from steps 1 and 2. Continue to draw his facial features. Add details to his sleeves and the back of his shirt.

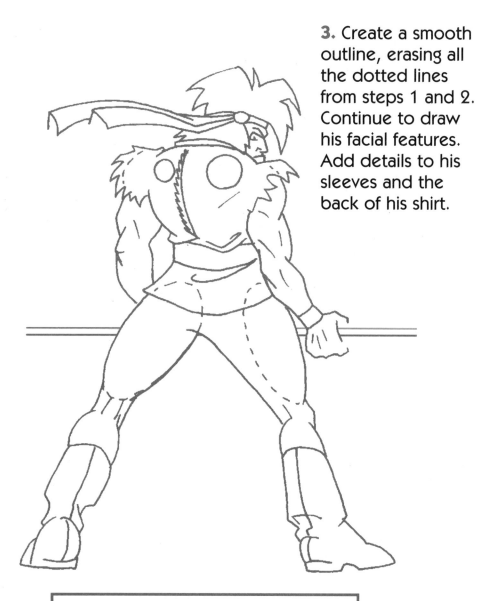

Tip: If you are not satisfied with the way any part of your drawing looks, erase it and start over.

4. Add all the finishing details. Darken all the areas shown. Now color Eric Staffman your favorite colors, and he'll be ready to defend the world!

Marielle Moonbeam

1. To start Marielle, draw a large, upside-down teardrop shape for the hair. Next, add a medium-sized oval for her upper body and a larger oval for her lower body. Continue adding guideline shapes for her head, arms, hands, knees, and feet. Then connect those shapes with lines.

Tip: Marielle may appear difficult to draw, but if you follow along carefully, step by step, you will be able to draw almost anything. It takes patience, practice, and lots of erasing to get it just right!

2. Using your guidelines from step 1, add facial features. Draw more ovals to fill out the arms and legs. Sketch in the boots and one glove. Give her a collar, and add a line on the right for a wall. Note the small triangle at the bottom of her hair.

3. Continue adding details to Marielle's eyes. Draw her sleeves, shorts, belt, buttons, and other glove. Remember to keep erasing unneeded lines as you go along.

4. Shade in her neck and eyes. Erase all dotted lines from step 3 and add the final touches to her clothing and hair. (Note the star on her boots.)

Gory the Gladiator

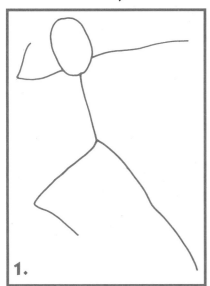

1.

1. & 2. Begin by lightly drawing the basic line figure. Then add the overlapping ovals and other guideline body shapes.

Tip: Draw these key steps carefully. Get the stick figure to gesture in the directions you want it to. By carefully adding the ovals over the stick figure, you will create a solid foundation.

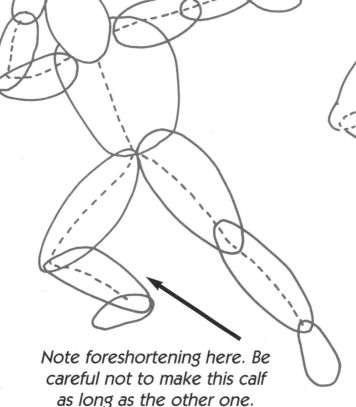

Note foreshortening here. Be careful not to make this calf as long as the other one.

3. Start defining the muscles within the oval guidelines and add guideline shapes for Gory the Gladiator's cape, clothes, and head-gear. Erase any unneeded guidelines.

4. Blend the body shapes together as you continue adding the clothes. Outline the cape and skirted part of the tunic; then add the facial details, sword, and fingers.

5. Complete this superhero by adding lots of details to his outfit. When you are finished with that, why not add some hot colors for dramatic effect?

Dragon-slayer

1. Sketching lightly, draw an oval for a head, then a stick-figure body and legs. Add ovals for shoulders, hips, and knees, and basic shapes for the feet. Then sketch simple guidelines for the facial features and sword.

Note foreshortening

2. Draw the basic shape of his hair, then sketch in simple shapes for ear, eyes, nose, and mouth. Next, to form the body, draw lines connecting your basic shapes. Then draw fingers and the outlines of a sword in Dragon-slayer's right hand and a shield on his left side.

3. Start defining the face, body, clothing, and weapons, erasing unneeded guidelines as you go along. Sketch and erase until you are satisfied with this stage of your drawing, then make a clean outline of your figure.

4. Using a black pen or colored markers, add dramatic shadows, decorative details, and other finishing touches. For an exciting action scene, try creating a fierce, fire-breathing dragon for your hero to do battle with!

Tip: Feel free to use your imagination when completing an imaginary figure. Add whatever details you wish—and as many or as few as you like.

Nansu Dawn

2. Add more ovals for her ponytails, then begin to outline her hands. Lightly, start to sketch her facial features, cape, and collar.

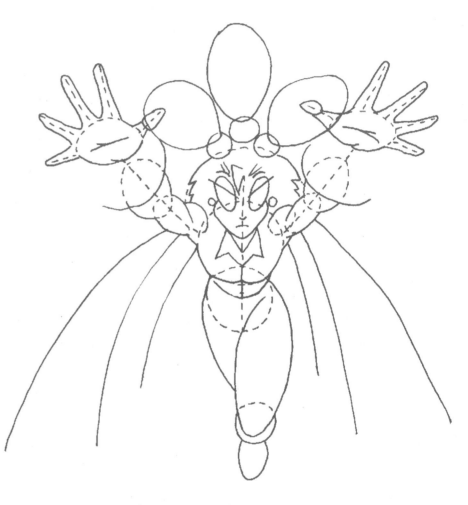

1. To begin drawing Nansu Dawn, draw two overlapping circles for her body. Add the ovals for her legs and arms. Next, add curved lines to start her cape, hair, and face. Don't forget the guidelines for her fingers.

Tip: If at this point you are not satisfied with any part of your drawing, erase it and start over.

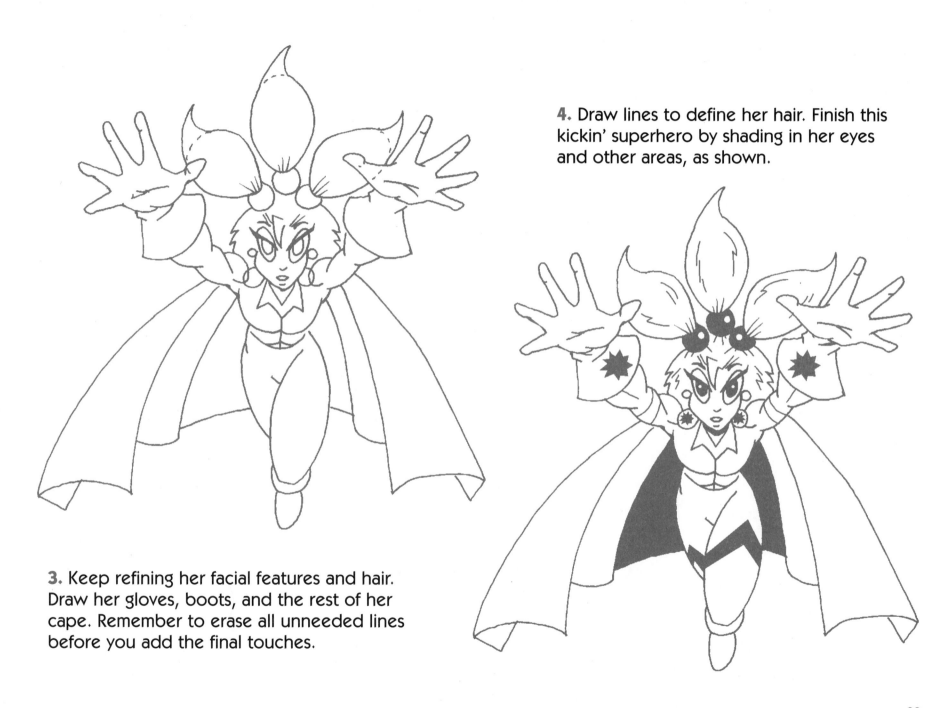

4. Draw lines to define her hair. Finish this kickin' superhero by shading in her eyes and other areas, as shown.

3. Keep refining her facial features and hair. Draw her gloves, boots, and the rest of her cape. Remember to erase all unneeded lines before you add the final touches.

Bolt-man

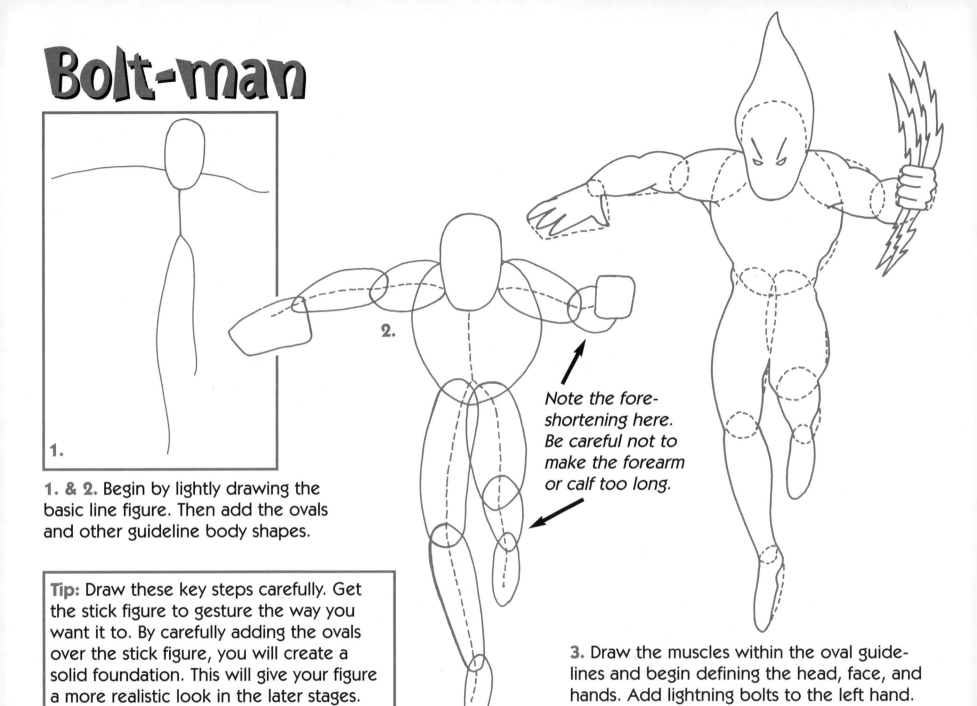

1. & 2. Begin by lightly drawing the basic line figure. Then add the ovals and other guideline body shapes.

2.

Note the fore-shortening here. Be careful not to make the forearm or calf too long.

Tip: Draw these key steps carefully. Get the stick figure to gesture the way you want it to. By carefully adding the ovals over the stick figure, you will create a solid foundation. This will give your figure a more realistic look in the later stages.

3. Draw the muscles within the oval guide-lines and begin defining the head, face, and hands. Add lightning bolts to the left hand.

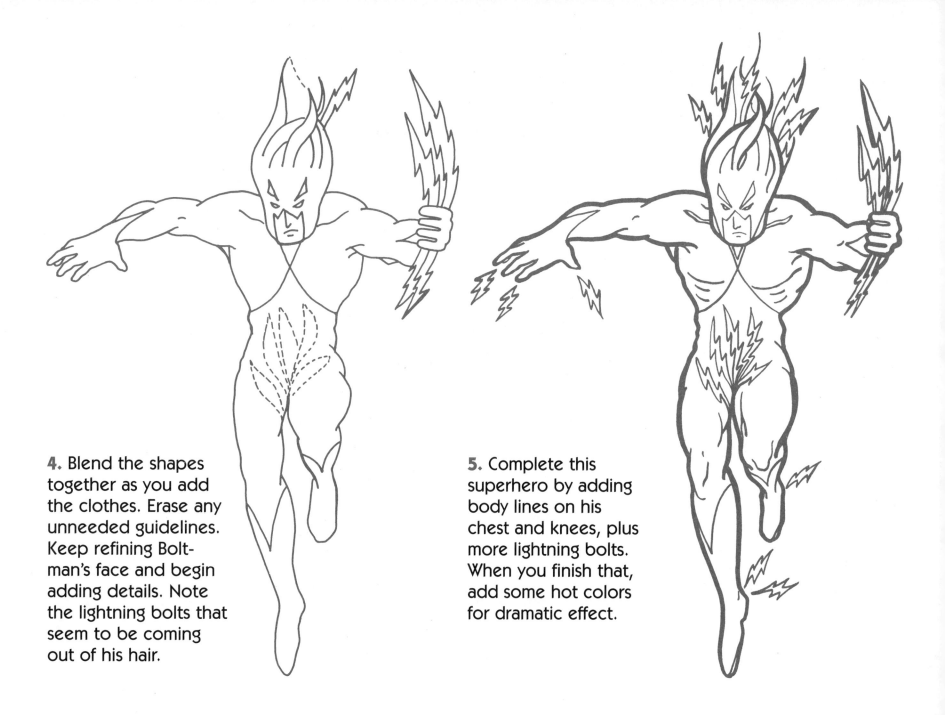

4. Blend the shapes together as you add the clothes. Erase any unneeded guidelines. Keep refining Bolt-man's face and begin adding details. Note the lightning bolts that seem to be coming out of his hair.

5. Complete this superhero by adding body lines on his chest and knees, plus more lightning bolts. When you finish that, add some hot colors for dramatic effect.

Ivan Stormchaser

1. Draw a stick figure to use as a guideline for the rest of your character. Add ovals for his body, head, feet, and arms. Sketch the guidelines for his face and a curved line over his head to start the horns on his helmet.

Remember: Keep your lines lightly drawn. They will be easier to erase when you no longer need them.

2. Draw the horns on his hat, then begin designing his facial features and hair. Using your stick figure from step 1 as a guideline, create an outline for the rest of his body. Draw crooked lines from his neck to start his cape.

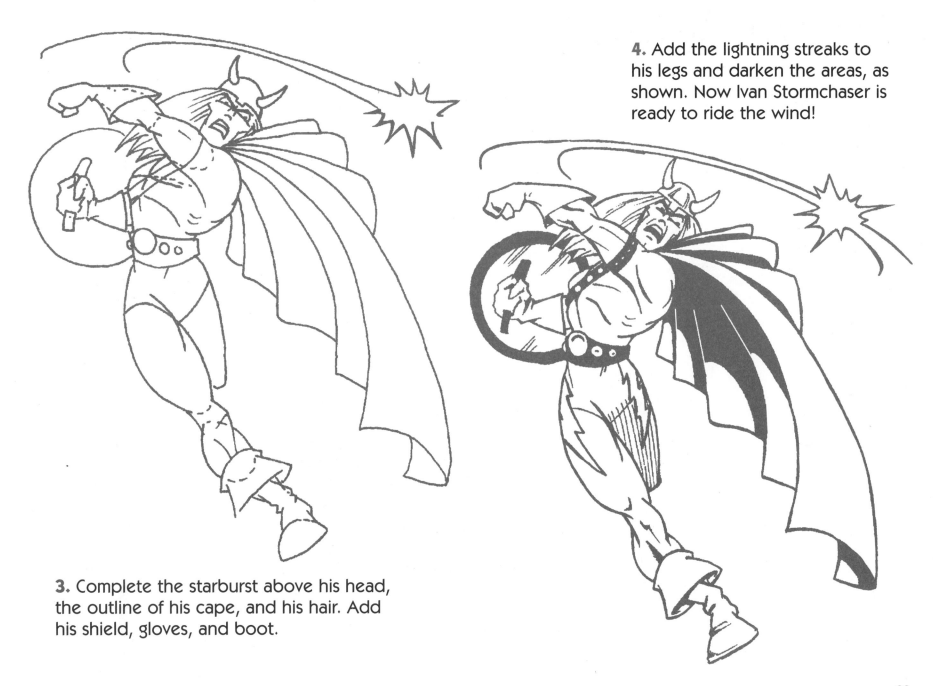

4. Add the lightning streaks to his legs and darken the areas, as shown. Now Ivan Stormchaser is ready to ride the wind!

3. Complete the starburst above his head, the outline of his cape, and his hair. Add his shield, gloves, and boot.

Jantra Adon

1. This animated warrior princess is started with a stick figure. Add circles and ovals for her body, head, arms, shield, and staff. Then add shapes for her feet and knees.

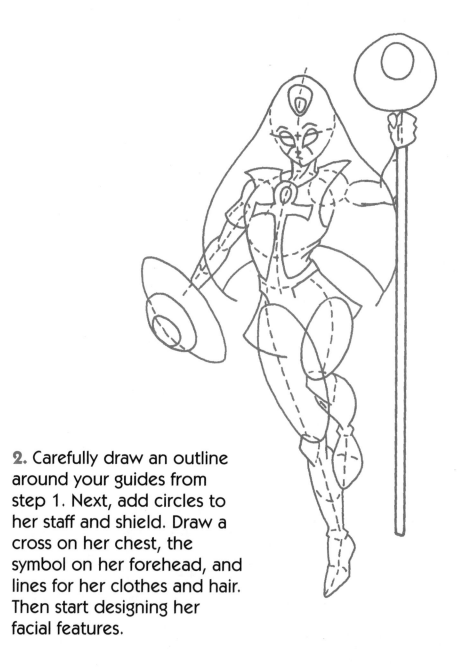

2. Carefully draw an outline around your guides from step 1. Next, add circles to her staff and shield. Draw a cross on her chest, the symbol on her forehead, and lines for her clothes and hair. Then start designing her facial features.

3. Add the rest of the handle on Jantra Adon's staff. Keep refining her facial features, hair, clothes, and shield.

4. Make sure that you have erased all unneeded guidelines. Add the finishing touches to her clothes and shield. Shade the areas shown, and Jantra Adon will be ready to protect you.

Falconer

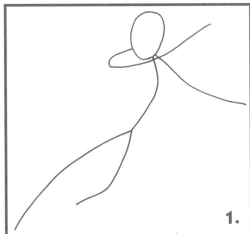

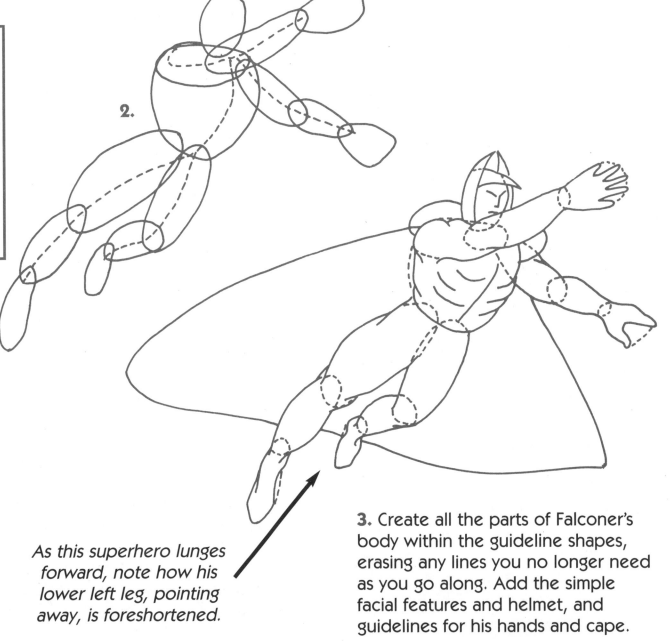

1. & 2. Starting with the oval-shaped head, draw the stick figure. Add the broad body shapes for the muscular arms, legs, and chest. Remember to keep all guidelines lightly drawn.

Tip: Superheroes usually have exaggerated muscle lines that make them appear powerful.

As this superhero lunges forward, note how his lower left leg, pointing away, is foreshortened.

3. Create all the parts of Falconer's body within the guideline shapes, erasing any lines you no longer need as you go along. Add the simple facial features and helmet, and guidelines for his hands and cape.

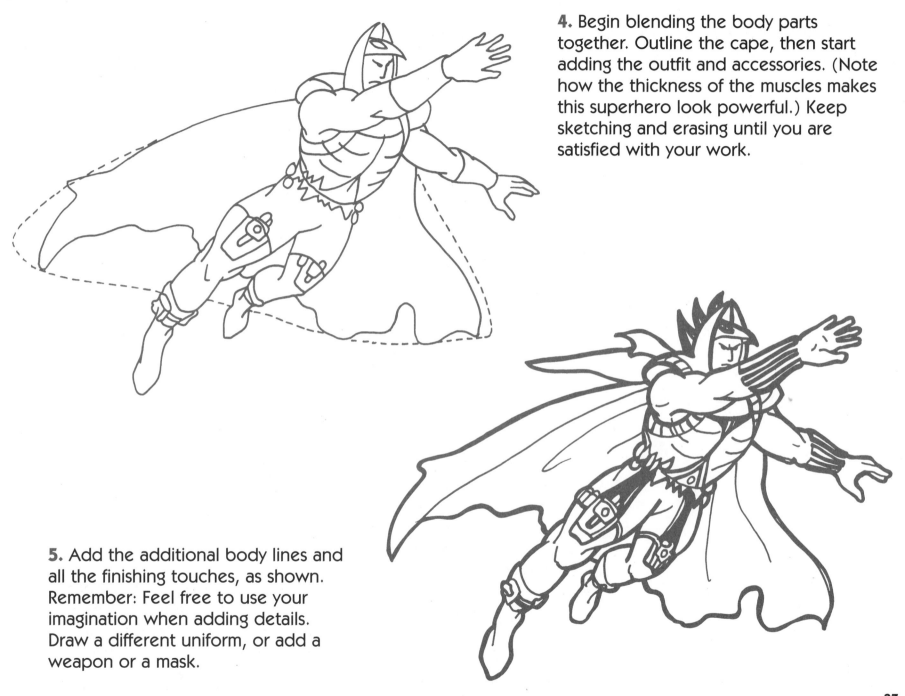

4. Begin blending the body parts together. Outline the cape, then start adding the outfit and accessories. (Note how the thickness of the muscles makes this superhero look powerful.) Keep sketching and erasing until you are satisfied with your work.

5. Add the additional body lines and all the finishing touches, as shown. Remember: Feel free to use your imagination when adding details. Draw a different uniform, or add a weapon or a mask.

Angela Windwalker

1. Start this anime character with a stick figure. Add ovals for her arms, chest, head, and hair. Draw the other shapes, as shown, for her feet, knees, and hands. Sketching lightly, draw guidelines for her facial features.

Tip: Steps 1 and 2 are very important. They establish the basic structure and overall look of your drawing. In steps 3 and 4, you will refine and add details to the figure that you created in steps 1 and 2.

2. Using your guidelines, create an outline. Lightly sketch in the outline for the wings. Add the skirt and the hair around her face.

3. Erase the guidelines you no longer need from steps 1 and 2, then add a layer of feathers under the skirt. Keep adding details to this character's face, wings, and clothes. Sketch in her boots and long hair.

4. Carefully, draw in the feathers on her wings. Then shade in her outfit, paying close attention to the designs on her arms. After you have done all the finishing touches, color Angela Windwalker, then create a sky for her to fly through.

Khaldar Turboboost

1. Carefully draw the oval for Khaldar's chest. Next, add the ovals that create his arms and legs. Take your time, making sure that you follow the size and shape of each oval carefully. This will make it easier to draw in his muscles later. Then sketch guideline shapes for his head and his turbo pack.

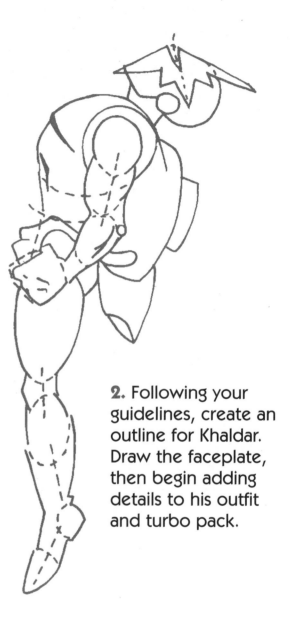

2. Following your guidelines, create an outline for Khaldar. Draw the faceplate, then begin adding details to his outfit and turbo pack.

Tip: Take your time doing steps 1 and 2. If you get the basic foundation right, the rest of your drawing will be easier to do.

3. Erase the dotted lines from step 2. Darken the area for his eyes. Add more details to the turbo pack.

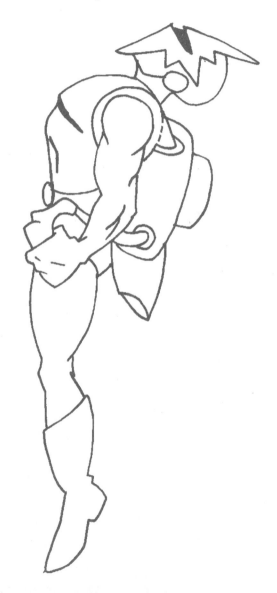

4. Add the finishing touches to Khaldar's turbo pack, outfit, and muscles. Don't forget the three lines that show how fast he is flying!

Lektra

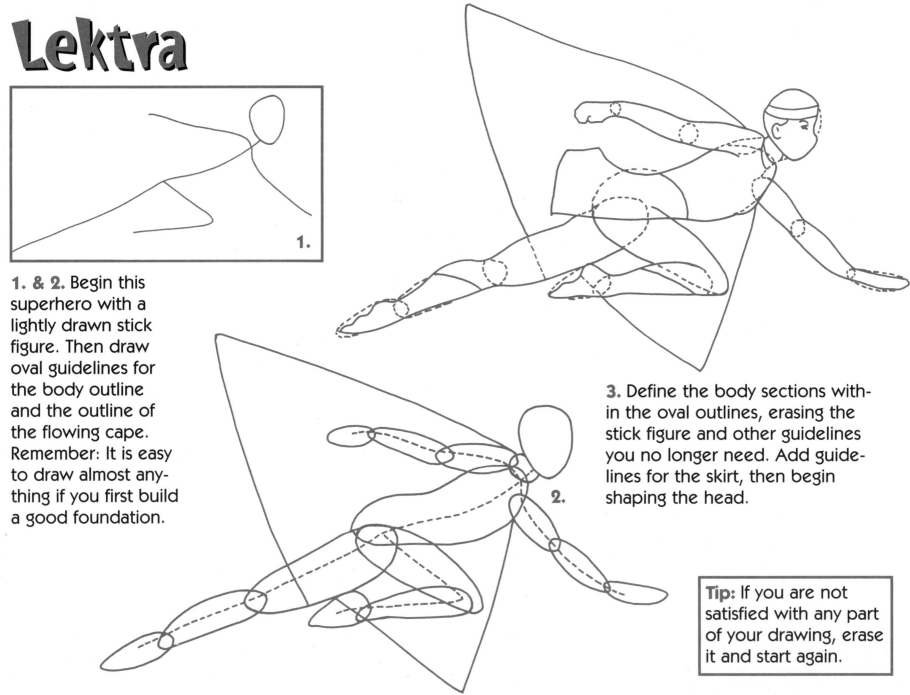

1.

2.

1. & 2. Begin this superhero with a lightly drawn stick figure. Then draw oval guidelines for the body outline and the outline of the flowing cape. Remember: It is easy to draw almost anything if you first build a good foundation.

3. Define the body sections within the oval outlines, erasing the stick figure and other guidelines you no longer need. Add guidelines for the skirt, then begin shaping the head.

Tip: If you are not satisfied with any part of your drawing, erase it and start again.

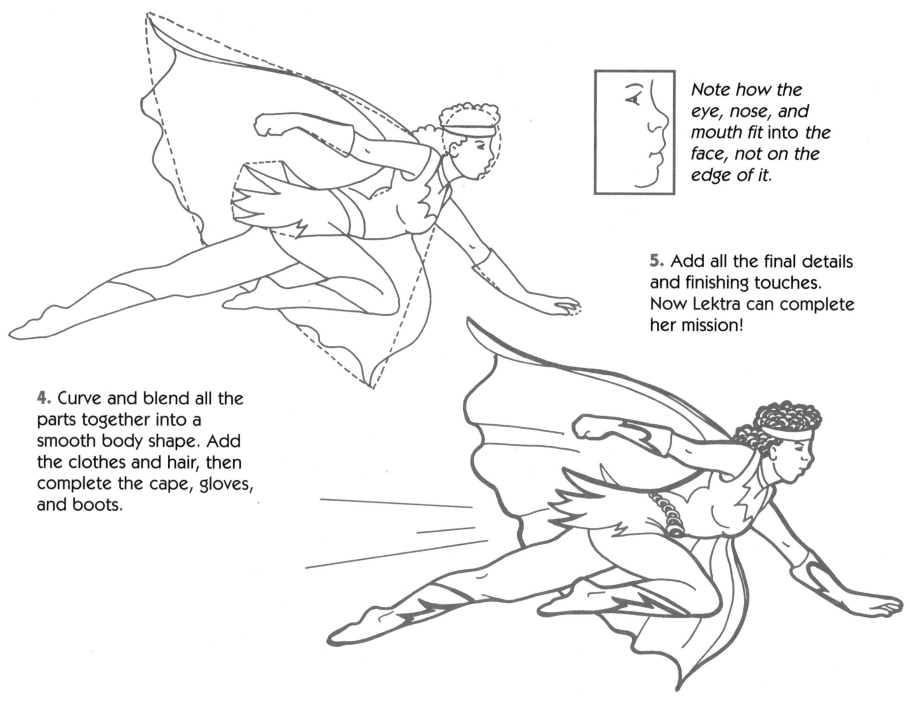

Note how the eye, nose, and mouth fit into the face, not on the edge of it.

5. Add all the final details and finishing touches. Now Lektra can complete her mission!

4. Curve and blend all the parts together into a smooth body shape. Add the clothes and hair, then complete the cape, gloves, and boots.

Rahab the Red

1. Carefully draw a stick figure. Add the ovals for the head, body, and legs, and sketch the guidelines for her ears and facial features.

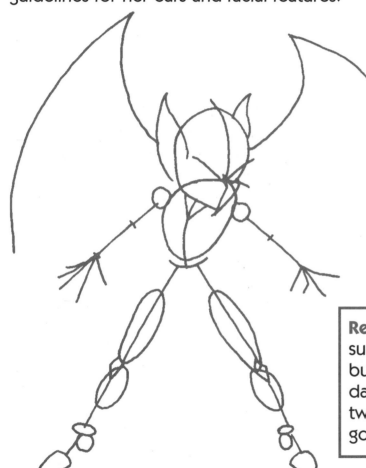

Remember: Make sure that you have built a solid foundation with the first two steps before going on to step 3.

2. Carefully outline the ovals and stick figure. Refine her facial features, then start sketching in her boots, clothes, and wings. Take your time with this step.

3. Finish Rahab the Red's wings and boots. Keep refining her facial features, hair, and clothes.

4. For the finishing touches, add more details to Rahab's clothes and facial features. Shade in her hair and other areas, as shown. Don't forget the lines that show how fast she can fly!

Mighty Zankon

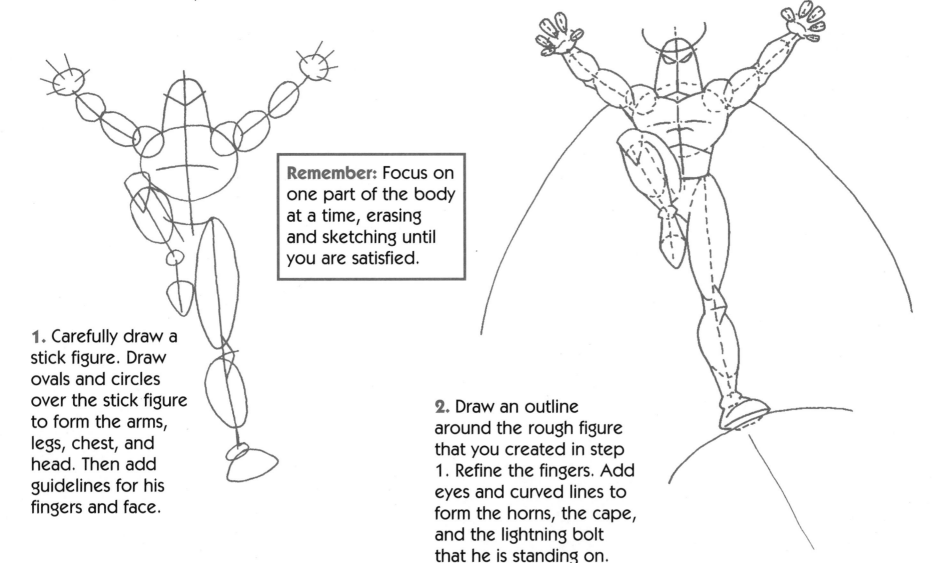

Remember: Focus on one part of the body at a time, erasing and sketching until you are satisfied.

1. Carefully draw a stick figure. Draw ovals and circles over the stick figure to form the arms, legs, chest, and head. Then add guidelines for his fingers and face.

2. Draw an outline around the rough figure that you created in step 1. Refine the fingers. Add eyes and curved lines to form the horns, the cape, and the lightning bolt that he is standing on.

3. Refine the Mighty Zankon's horns, facial features, and lightning bolt. Add two circles on his chest with lines going over his shoulders. Draw a few lines to create his cape, and add a crisscross pattern on his boots. Notice the contour lines on his chest.

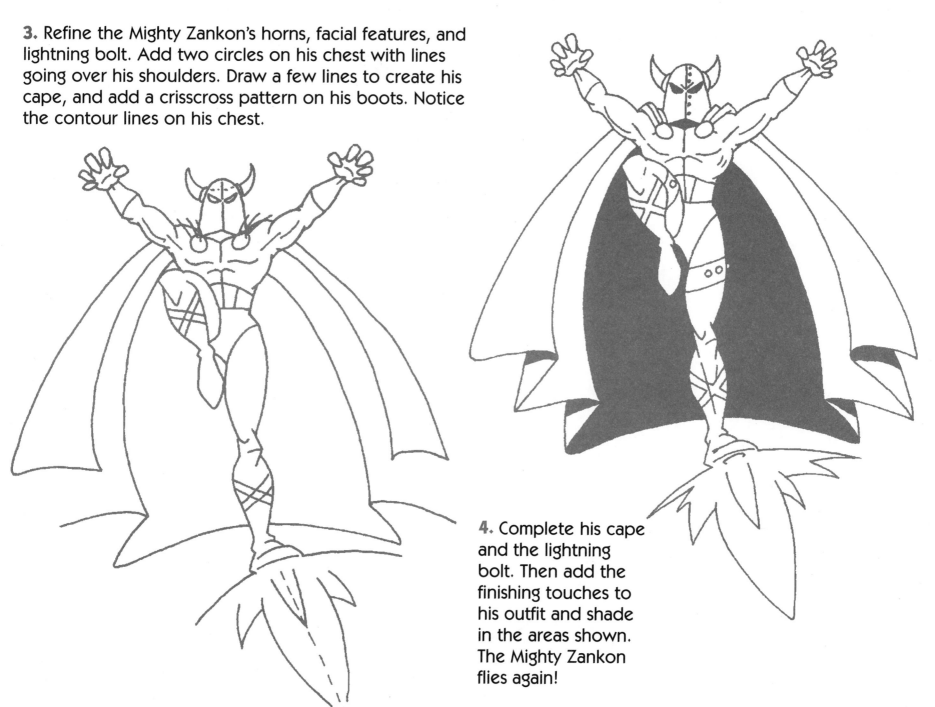

4. Complete his cape and the lightning bolt. Then add the finishing touches to his outfit and shade in the areas shown. The Mighty Zankon flies again!

Jason of the Argonauts

1. Start with this simple, lightly sketched stick figure.

2. Draw ovals at the shoulders, elbows, and knees. Then sketch basic shapes for the hands and feet.

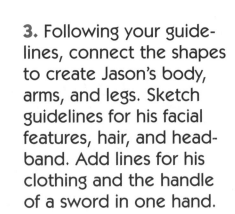

3. Following your guidelines, connect the shapes to create Jason's body, arms, and legs. Sketch guidelines for his facial features, hair, and headband. Add lines for his clothing and the handle of a sword in one hand.

5. Add the final details to Jason's facial features. Then fill in (or color) his hair and clothing and add other finishing touches. Using shadows and thicker outlines will make his body pop out of the background. This hero is all set to go!

Tip: Add details and finishing touches only *after* you have blended and refined the shapes and your figure is complete.

4. Draw more of the clothing and sword, erasing unneeded guidelines. Sketch and erase until you get the body and clothing the way you want them. Then draw the hair and facial features. Sketch guidelines for the wall on which Jason stands.

Power Puncher

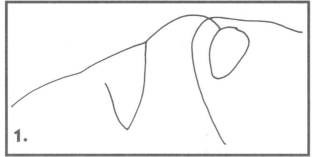

1.

1. & 2. Lightly draw the gesturing stick figure and all the overlapping guideline shapes around it.

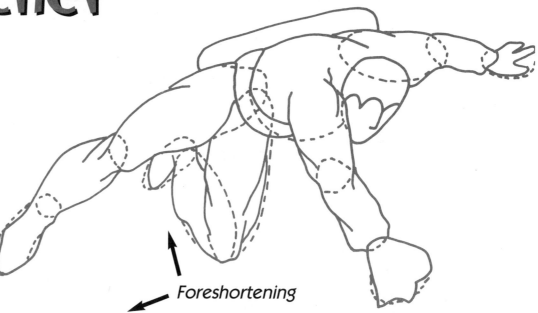

Foreshortening

2.

Remember: Use foreshortening when any part of the body points away from you, the viewer. This will give your figure a dramatic, three-dimensional look.

3. Within the ovals, create the muscular legs and outline the clothing on his upper body. Erase the stick-figure guideline as you go along. Start defining the left hand, as well as the power pack on the right one.

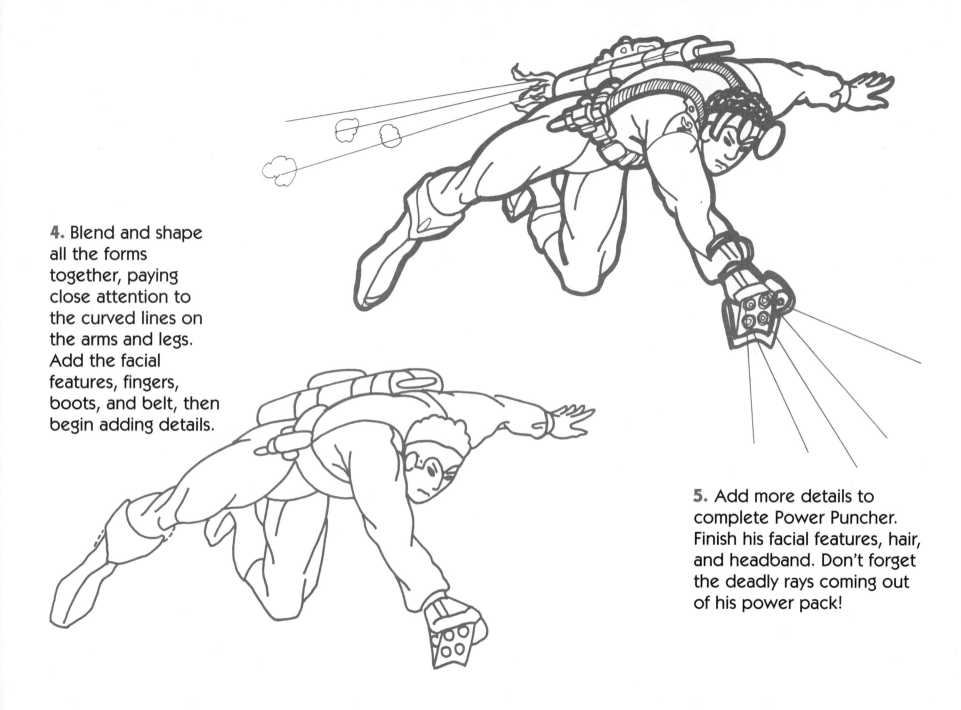

4. Blend and shape all the forms together, paying close attention to the curved lines on the arms and legs. Add the facial features, fingers, boots, and belt, then begin adding details.

5. Add more details to complete Power Puncher. Finish his facial features, hair, and headband. Don't forget the deadly rays coming out of his power pack!

Veshti Vanu

1. Begin by drawing a large backward C (or an irregular oval, open on one side) to start the helmet. Form the face by sketching an overlapping heart shape that is jagged on one side. (The jagged line creates a cheekbone.) Then, sketching lightly, create guidelines for the nose, eyes, mouth, and neck by adding simple lines, as shown.

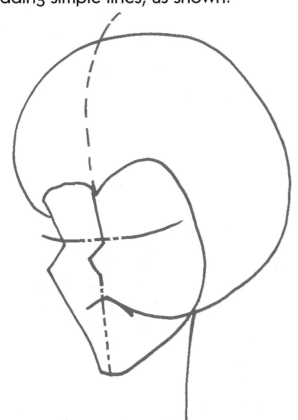

2. Add details to Veshti Vanu's facial features, and make her outline smooth. Sketch the designs on her helmet and her microphone. Then start drawing her clothes.

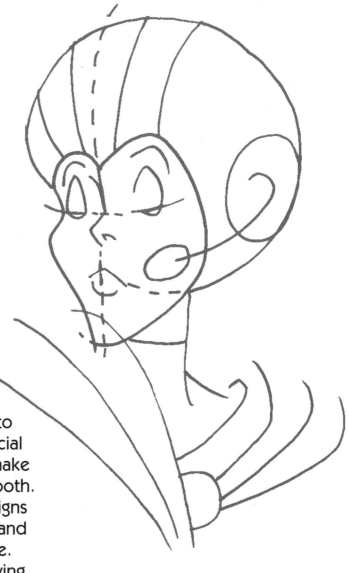

Remember: Make sure that you have built a solid foundation with the first two steps before going on to step 3.

3. Continue refining this character's facial features, microphone, and helmet. Note the lines on her neck.

4. Complete your designs on her helmet, and shade in her eyes, neck, and mouth.

Princess Sword

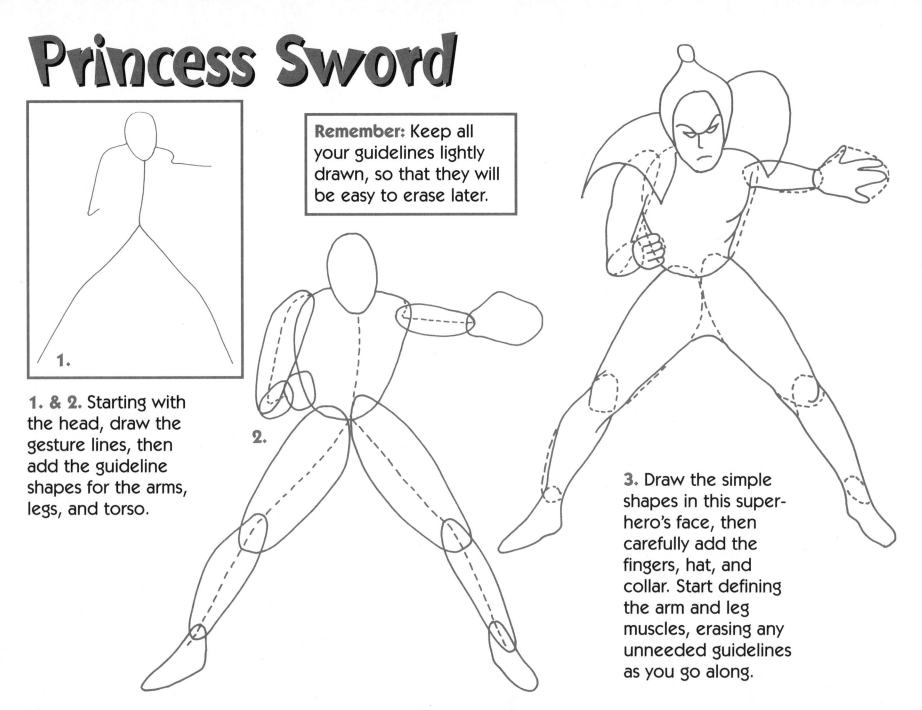

1.

1. & 2. Starting with the head, draw the gesture lines, then add the guideline shapes for the arms, legs, and torso.

2.

Remember: Keep all your guidelines lightly drawn, so that they will be easy to erase later.

3. Draw the simple shapes in this super-hero's face, then carefully add the fingers, hat, and collar. Start defining the arm and leg muscles, erasing any unneeded guidelines as you go along.

54

4. Complete the facial features, hands, and fingers. Blend the parts together and add the clothes and sword. Then begin adding details as shown. Keep erasing and drawing until you are satisfied with your drawing.

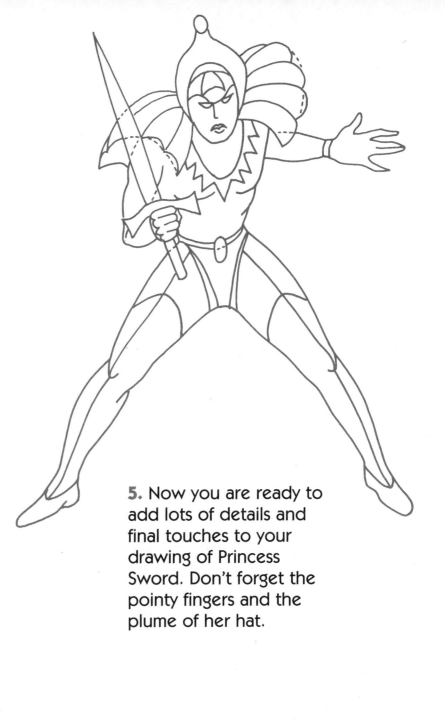

5. Now you are ready to add lots of details and final touches to your drawing of Princess Sword. Don't forget the pointy fingers and the plume of her hat.

Lightning Lorac

1. Draw the large oval in the middle first. Slowly, add the overlapping ovals and connecting lines. Take your time, working on one area at a time.

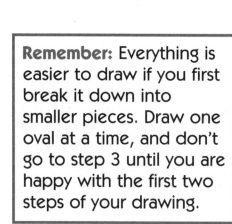

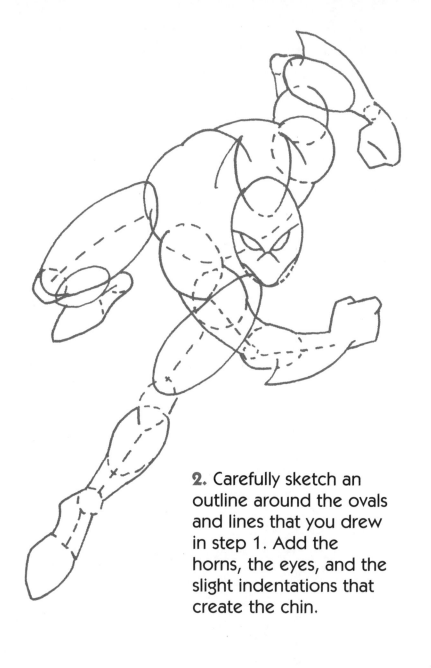

Remember: Everything is easier to draw if you first break it down into smaller pieces. Draw one oval at a time, and don't go to step 3 until you are happy with the first two steps of your drawing.

2. Carefully sketch an outline around the ovals and lines that you drew in step 1. Add the horns, the eyes, and the slight indentations that create the chin.

3. Erase all of the dotted guidelines from step 2. This will create a smooth, clean outline. Note that some lines are left to form muscles, as in his shoulders. Finish the horns.

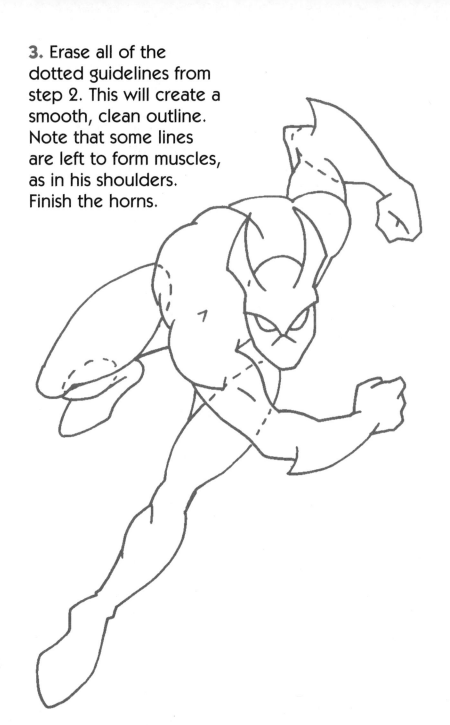

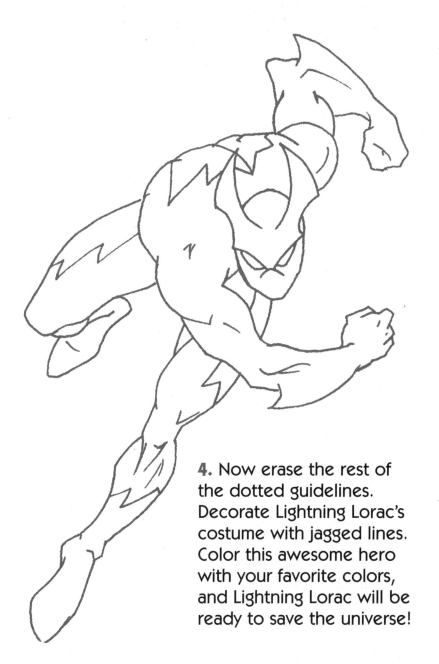

4. Now erase the rest of the dotted guidelines. Decorate Lightning Lorac's costume with jagged lines. Color this awesome hero with your favorite colors, and Lightning Lorac will be ready to save the universe!

Kid Tempest

1. Start by drawing an oval shape with a pointy bottom. Add a small, tear-shaped oval for the ear. About midway to the chin, draw a neck line. Then lightly sketch some guidelines to help you place the facial features.

2. Add lines for the hair, and begin drawing the eyes, mouth, and neck. Erase guidelines as you go along.

Tip: Dotted lines represent guidelines that you will erase later, when they are no longer needed.

3. Complete the eyebrows, ear, mouth, and nose. Refine the shape of the head and hair.

4. Refine the face, darken the eyes, and Kid Tempest will be ready to storm after any villain!

Quasar-man

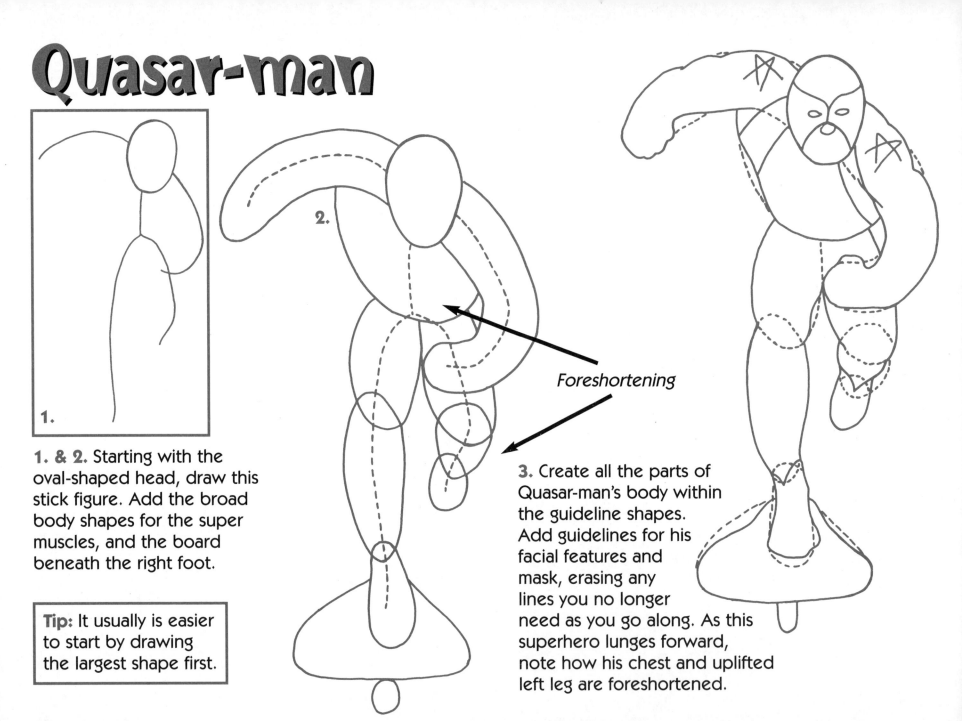

1. & 2. Starting with the oval-shaped head, draw this stick figure. Add the broad body shapes for the super muscles, and the board beneath the right foot.

Tip: It usually is easier to start by drawing the largest shape first.

2.

Foreshortening

3. Create all the parts of Quasar-man's body within the guideline shapes. Add guidelines for his facial features and mask, erasing any lines you no longer need as you go along. As this superhero lunges forward, note how his chest and uplifted left leg are foreshortened.

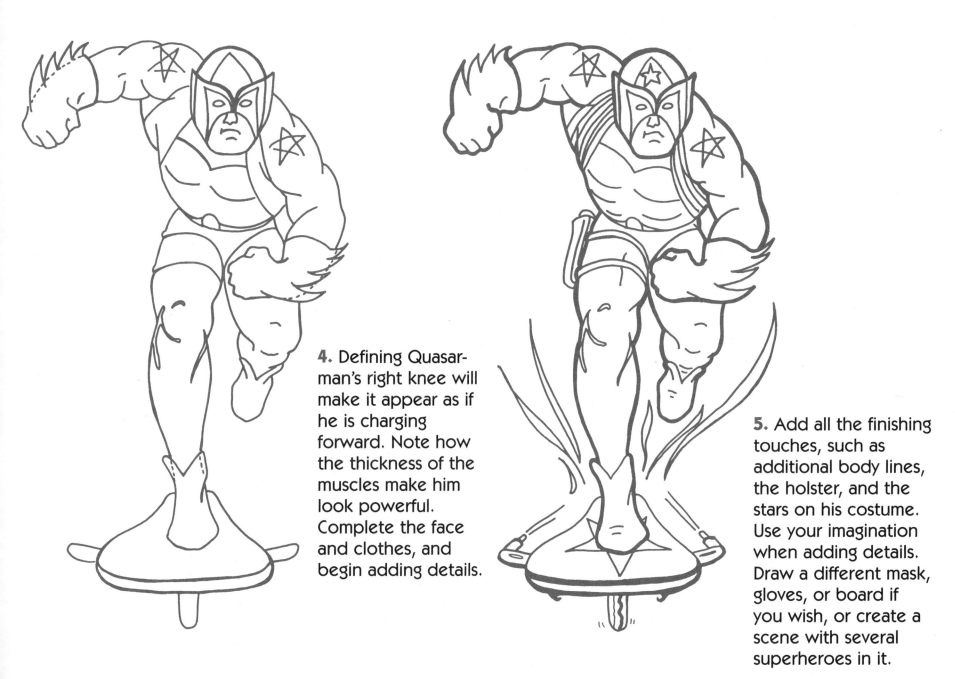

4. Defining Quasar-man's right knee will make it appear as if he is charging forward. Note how the thickness of the muscles make him look powerful. Complete the face and clothes, and begin adding details.

5. Add all the finishing touches, such as additional body lines, the holster, and the stars on his costume. Use your imagination when adding details. Draw a different mask, gloves, or board if you wish, or create a scene with several superheroes in it.

Lana Laserblast

1. Draw a stick figure. Add ovals to form the chest, arms, legs, and head. Draw free-form shapes for the hair and feet.

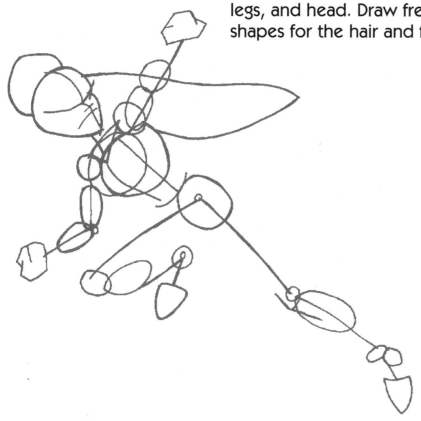

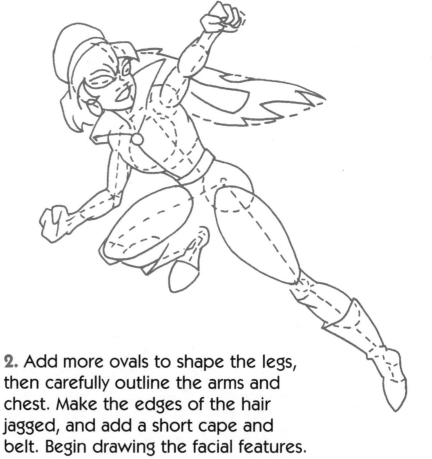

2. Add more ovals to shape the legs, then carefully outline the arms and chest. Make the edges of the hair jagged, and add a short cape and belt. Begin drawing the facial features.

3. Keep refining the hair, facial features, and outfit. Draw in the power spheres around this superhero's fists. Notice her boots and the clasps for her short cape.

Remember: If you are not satisfied with any part of your drawing, erase it and start over.

4. Finish the power spheres around her fists. Add the finishing touches to her cape, outfit, and headband. After you shade in the areas shown, Lana Laserblast will be ready to battle the forces of evil!

Reflectron

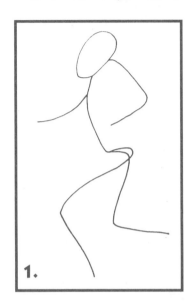

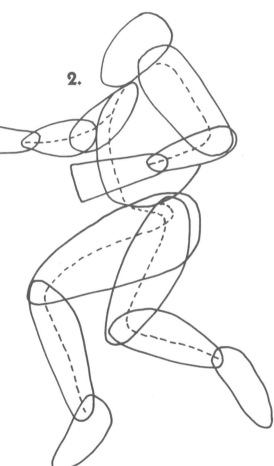

2.

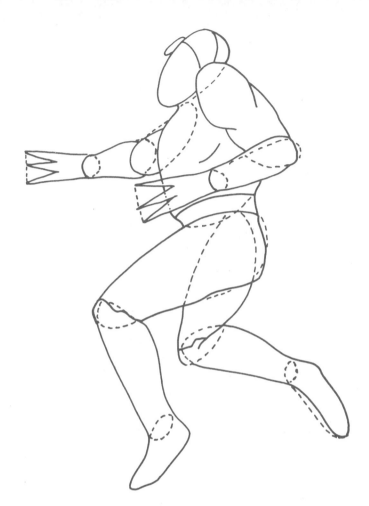

1. & 2. Draw the basic stick figure, then add over-lapping shapes to form body guidelines, as shown. Note that these are different shapes and sizes. (All, except for the hand shapes, are ovals.) Draw these shapes carefully. This will make it easier to create muscle shapes within them.

3. Define the body shapes within the oval guidelines, carefully erasing the stick figure and other unneeded guidelines as you go along.

5. Complete this superhero by adding more defining body lines and all the details.

4. Blend and smooth all the shapes together. Add clothing and the reflectors on his knees, belt, elbow, shoulder, and head. Since this figure is looking away, only a small profile of his face can be seen.

Tip: To create the reflection lines fanning out from the reflectors, first lightly sketch lines where you want them. Then go over them using a ruler to make them straight and smooth.

Garik Kickmaster

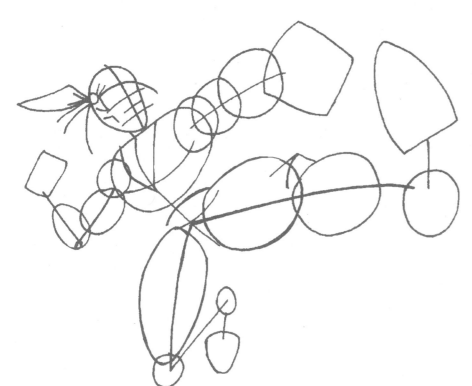

1. Draw a stick figure with its foot out. Add ovals for the head, chest, arms, and legs. Lightly, sketch in free-form shapes for the feet, hands, and bandanna. Add the guidelines for the face and hair.

2. Draw the heel to his boot and a circle on his bandanna. Then begin adding facial features. Carefully following your guideline shapes from step 1, outline the body and hair. Sketch in the shirt, belt, and wrist guards.

3. Add a jagged line of hair on his forehead and continue to refine his facial features. Add details to his shirt, boots, and fists. Make sure that you erase all unneeded lines as you go along.

Remember: Use your imagination when adding details to imaginary characters like these. Add as many, or as few, details as you wish.

4. Finish adding details to his facial features, bandanna, and outfit. Shade in some areas, as shown. Garik Kickmaster is ready to show off his skills!

Robo-man

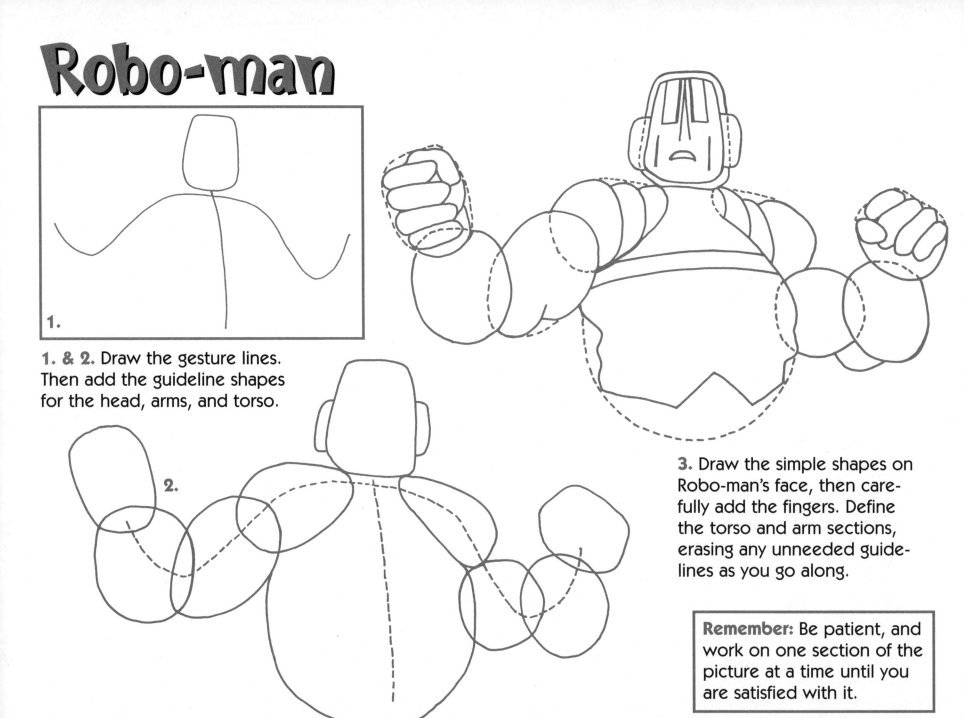

1.

1. & 2. Draw the gesture lines. Then add the guideline shapes for the head, arms, and torso.

2.

3. Draw the simple shapes on Robo-man's face, then carefully add the fingers. Define the torso and arm sections, erasing any unneeded guidelines as you go along.

Remember: Be patient, and work on one section of the picture at a time until you are satisfied with it.

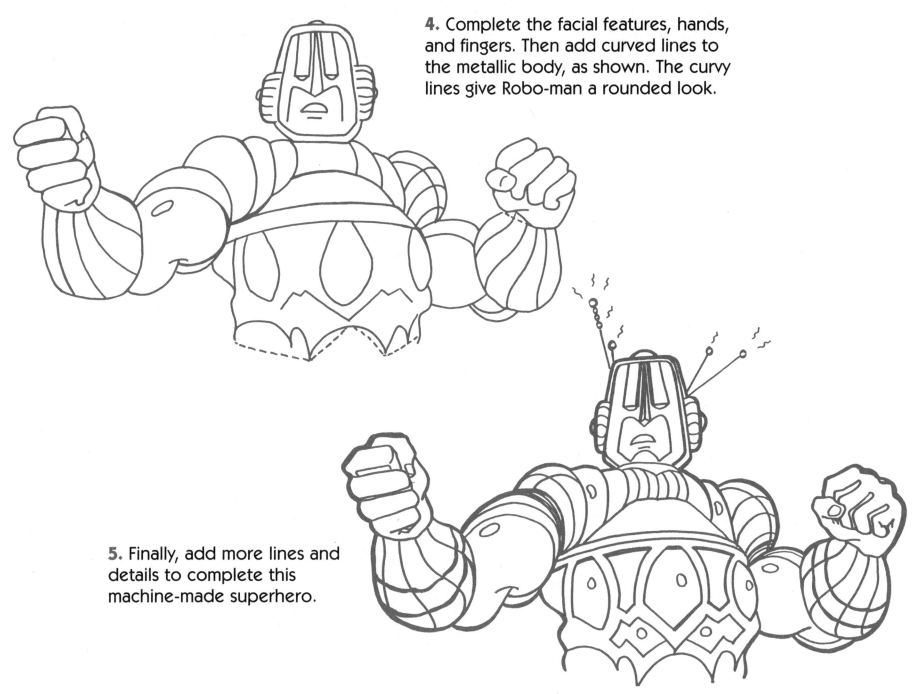

4. Complete the facial features, hands, and fingers. Then add curved lines to the metallic body, as shown. The curvy lines give Robo-man a rounded look.

5. Finally, add more lines and details to complete this machine-made superhero.

Luna Leigh

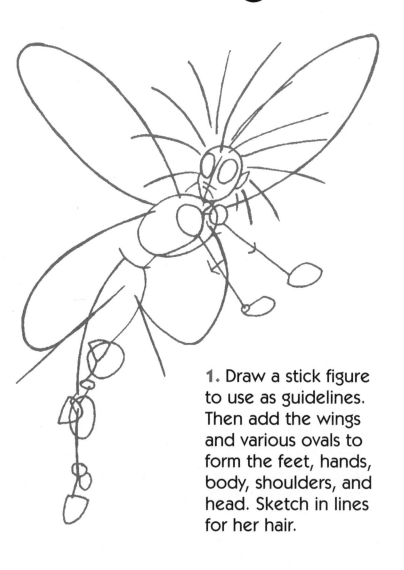

1. Draw a stick figure to use as guidelines. Then add the wings and various ovals to form the feet, hands, body, shoulders, and head. Sketch in lines for her hair.

2. Add another line around the wings. Then draw around the body ovals to create a more defined outline. Begin adding facial features and a belt.

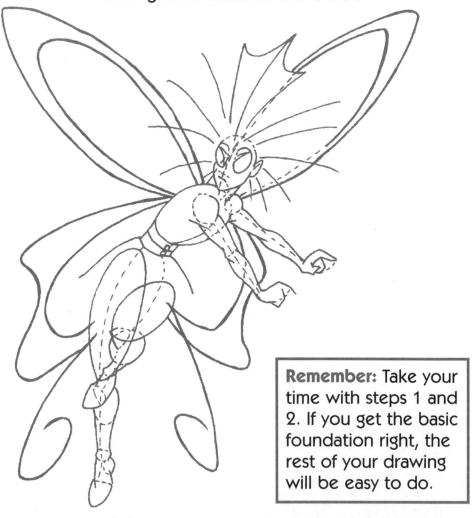

Remember: Take your time with steps 1 and 2. If you get the basic foundation right, the rest of your drawing will be easy to do.

4. Shade in Luna Leigh's eyes, the dot on her forehead, and other areas, as shown. Be sure to finish the bottom of her skirt.

3. Connect the lines for her hair. Add details to her wings and facial features.

Steelo the Ultimate

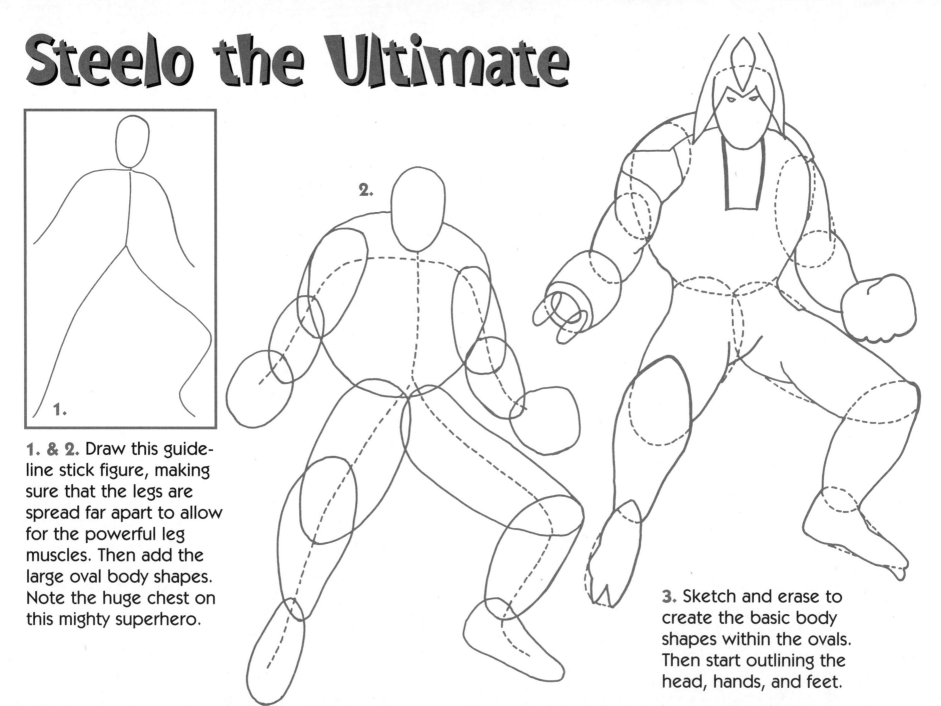

1.

2.

3.

1. & 2. Draw this guide-line stick figure, making sure that the legs are spread far apart to allow for the powerful leg muscles. Then add the large oval body shapes. Note the huge chest on this mighty superhero.

3. Sketch and erase to create the basic body shapes within the ovals. Then start outlining the head, hands, and feet.

72

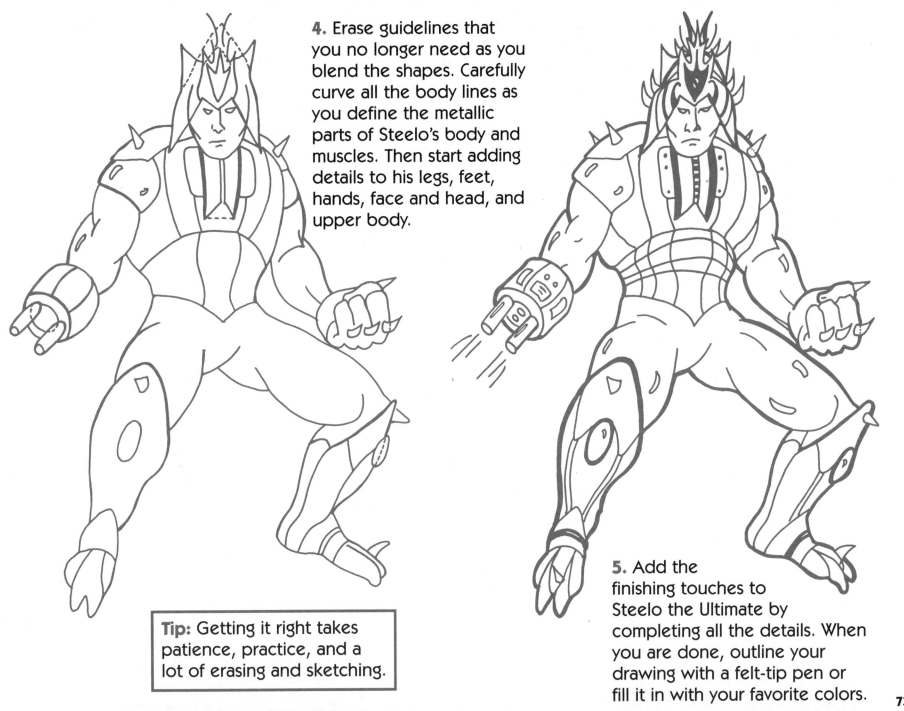

4. Erase guidelines that you no longer need as you blend the shapes. Carefully curve all the body lines as you define the metallic parts of Steelo's body and muscles. Then start adding details to his legs, feet, hands, face and head, and upper body.

Tip: Getting it right takes patience, practice, and a lot of erasing and sketching.

5. Add the finishing touches to Steelo the Ultimate by completing all the details. When you are done, outline your drawing with a felt-tip pen or fill it in with your favorite colors.

Mordecai Magicus

Remember: Use your imagination when-ever drawing an imaginary figure.

1. Start Mordecai Magicus by drawing a large oval for his body. Next, draw the guidelines for his face. Using those guidelines, begin to draw his facial features. Sketch in ovals and free-form shapes to start his hands, arms, legs, and feet. Then add a jagged line around his feet, as shown.

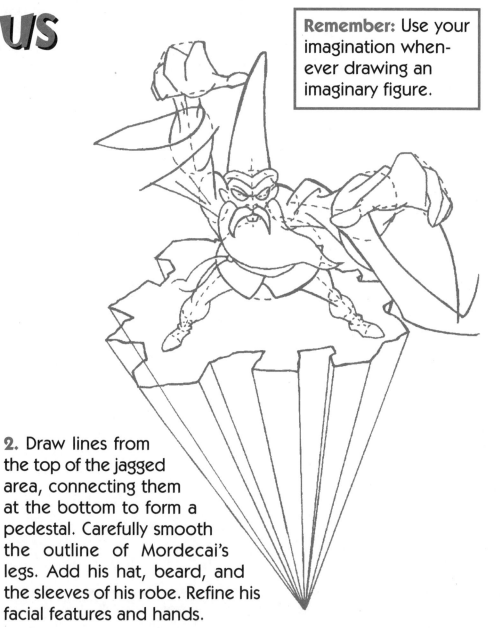

2. Draw lines from the top of the jagged area, connecting them at the bottom to form a pedestal. Carefully smooth the outline of Mordecai's legs. Add his hat, beard, and the sleeves of his robe. Refine his facial features and hands.

3. Add the spheres of power around Mordecai's hands and connect them with a jagged lightning line. Sketch and erase to give his beard a rough edge. Continue to refine his hands, robes, and facial features.

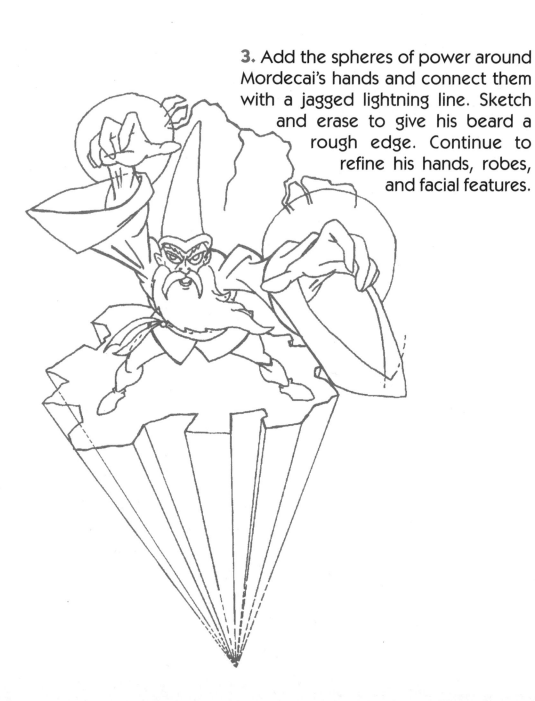

4. Add the final touches to the spheres and the lines connecting them. Begin adding the finishing touches. Notice his fingernails, the bottom of his pedestal, and the pictures on his hat. Shade in the areas shown. Mordecai Magicus, high on his pedestal, is ready for trouble!

Thora

Tip: Make sure that you have built a solid foundation in the first two steps before continuing.

1.

2.

1. & 2. Draw a simple stick figure in the action pose, as shown. Then add the various oval shapes. Note the rectangular guidelines for the hands.

3. Sketch the body parts within the oval guidelines, erasing unneeded guidelines as you go along. Begin forming Thora's hands and facial features, and create guidelines for her cape and flowing hair.

5. Finish Thora's hair and cape, and add all the final details that will make this superhero ready to spring into action.

4. Blend the body shapes and complete the hands and face. Then start forming her cape and long, flowing hair.

Transflier

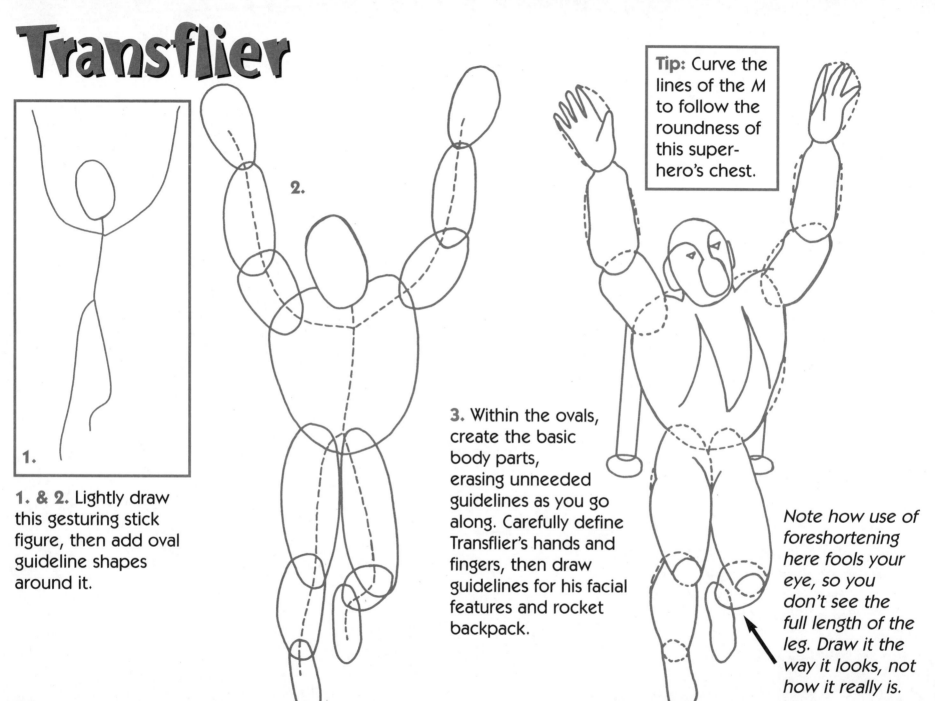

1.

1. & 2. Lightly draw this gesturing stick figure, then add oval guideline shapes around it.

2.

3. Within the ovals, create the basic body parts, erasing unneeded guidelines as you go along. Carefully define Transflier's hands and fingers, then draw guidelines for his facial features and rocket backpack.

Tip: Curve the lines of the *M* to follow the roundness of this super-hero's chest.

Note how use of foreshortening here fools your eye, so you don't see the full length of the leg. Draw it the way it looks, not how it really is.

4. Blend and shape all the forms together, paying close attention to the curved lines on the arms and legs. Continue working on the face and fingers, then begin adding details.

5. Add more details to complete Transflier. When you are finished, add exhaust lines to the rocket, showing how fast this superhero can zoom up and away.

Fairy

Tip: Studying the step 4 drawing before you start will help you understand what you are doing in steps 1, 2, and 3.

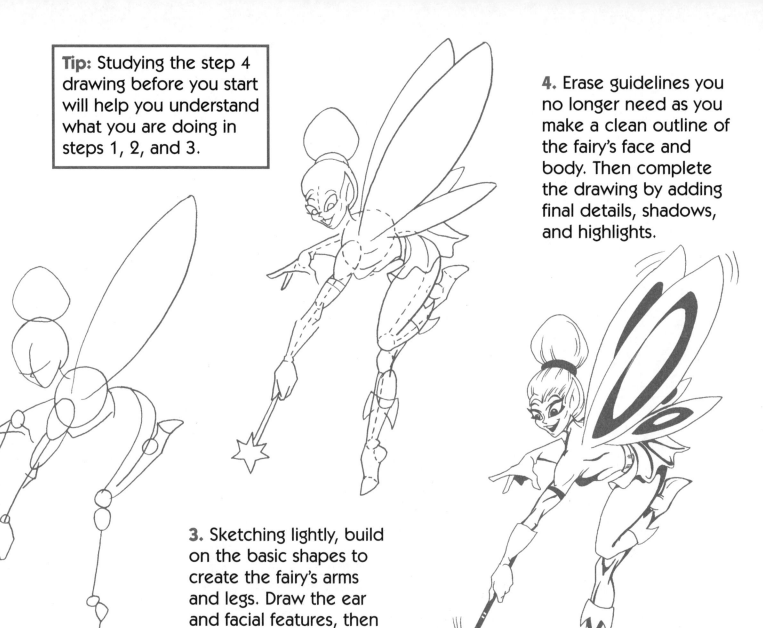

1. Start with this simple stick figure.

2. Add basic guideline shapes for shoulder, hands, feet, and joints.

3. Sketching lightly, build on the basic shapes to create the fairy's arms and legs. Draw the ear and facial features, then sketch in her wings, wand, dress, and boots.

4. Erase guidelines you no longer need as you make a clean outline of the fairy's face and body. Then complete the drawing by adding final details, shadows, and highlights.

Superhero sidekicks

Superheroes often have buddies, or sidekicks, who help them in their quests. Try drawing these few examples and adding them to your pictures. Then create more of your own.

Cyber Hunter

1. Begin by drawing a stick figure. Add a small upside-down heart for the top of the head, then draw the lines coming out of it. Lightly, add circles and ovals for the shoulders and knees. Next, add free-form shapes for the fingers, hands, and feet. Use lightly sketched lines to connect all the shapes.

Tip: This figure is harder than most, but be patient and work carefully on one area at a time. You will find that you are able to draw it.

2. Very carefully, outline the top part of the body. Use the lines around the head to create wings and horns. Then start sketching facial features and adding details to the hands, legs, and chest.

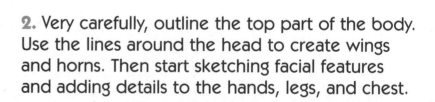

3. Continue to add details to the wings and facial features. Draw lines across the legs and arms, then add the leg armor and wrist guards. Notice the designs on the armor.

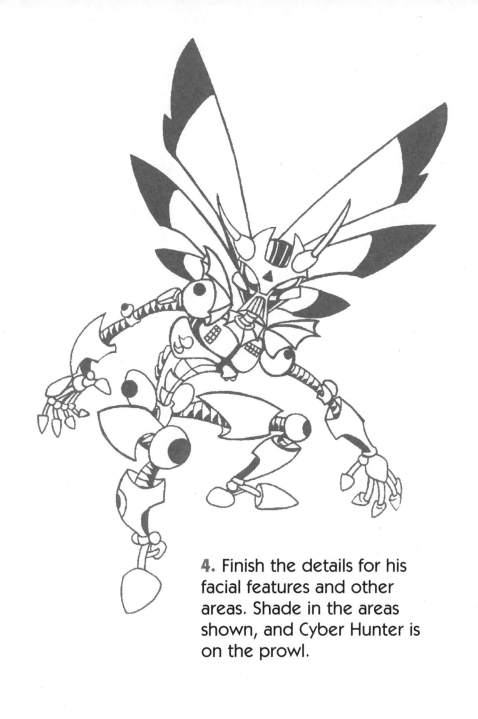

4. Finish the details for his facial features and other areas. Shade in the areas shown, and Cyber Hunter is on the prowl.

The Vapor Ranger

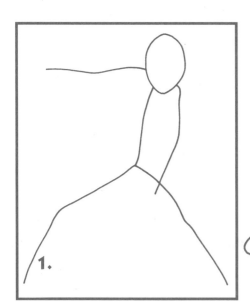

1.

Tip: It is easy to draw almost anything if you first break it down into simple shapes.

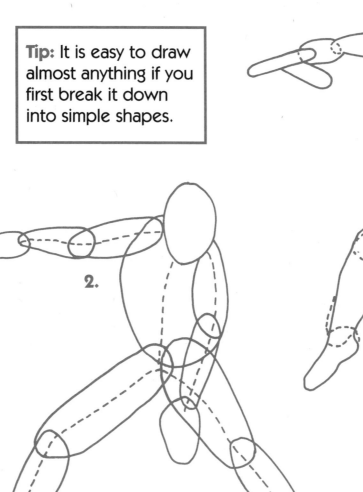

2.

1. & 2. Starting with the head, draw this simple stick figure. Then lightly sketch all the basic guideline body shapes, as shown.

3. Begin defining the arms and legs within the oval shapes. Start drawing the hands, feet, mask, and the Vapor Ranger's weapon.

4. Blend the shapes into a smooth body outline. Then add the costume, including the face mask and vapor sources on the shoulders and legs. After you complete the hands, feet, and weapon, start adding puffs of vapor.

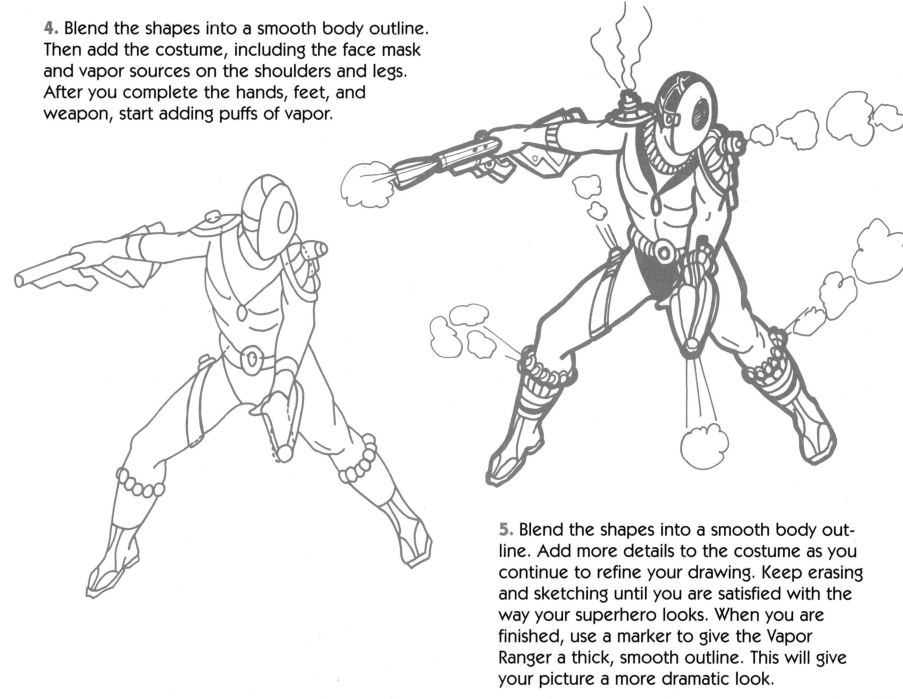

5. Blend the shapes into a smooth body outline. Add more details to the costume as you continue to refine your drawing. Keep erasing and sketching until you are satisfied with the way your superhero looks. When you are finished, use a marker to give the Vapor Ranger a thick, smooth outline. This will give your picture a more dramatic look.

Charyl Tombs

1. Start this character with a stick figure. Next, draw an oval for her head, then two circles on either side of the head, for her hair. Add guidelines to the face and begin sketching her facial features. Add simple, basic shapes for the feet, body, shoulders, and hands.

2. Outline the guide-line shapes that you created in step 1 to give shape and definition to the body. Create a jagged edge to the hair and add sunglasses to the face. Draw her bag, outfit, and shoe. Then take your time sketching in the walls around her.

3. Continue to refine the facial features. Add the strand of hair in front of her eyes, as well as details to the hair, clothes, bag, and walls. Notice her fingers on the wall to her right.

Remember: Practice makes perfect. Don't be discouraged if you can't draw this character right away. Just keep sketching and erasing until you can.

4. Add the finishing touches to her clothes. Then, working carefully, begin to shade in her eyes, her sunglasses, the walls, and the hole behind her. Charyl Tombs, extreme explorer, is now ready to explore the dark cave she has found!

Zantron

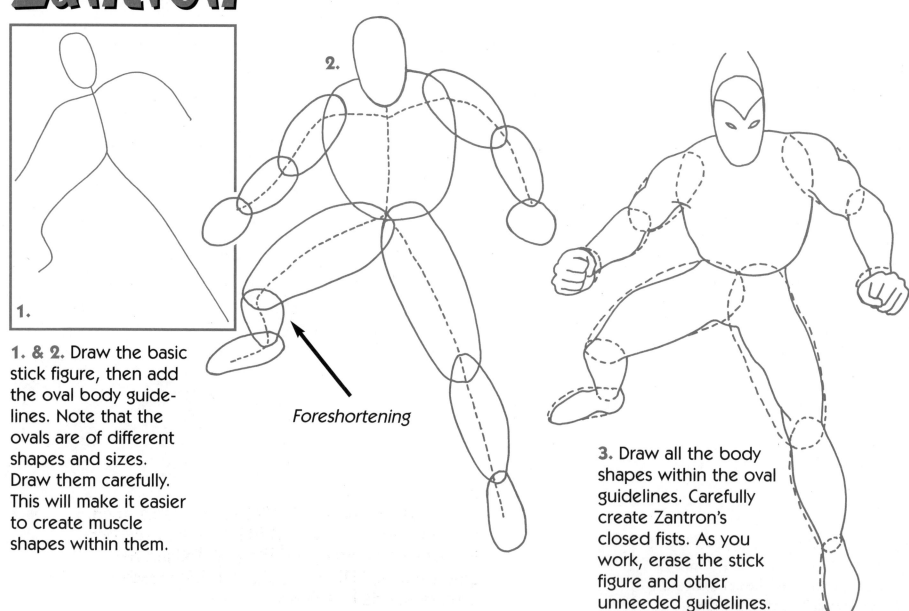

1. & 2. Draw the basic stick figure, then add the oval body guide-lines. Note that the ovals are of different shapes and sizes. Draw them carefully. This will make it easier to create muscle shapes within them.

Foreshortening

3. Draw all the body shapes within the oval guidelines. Carefully create Zantron's closed fists. As you work, erase the stick figure and other unneeded guidelines.

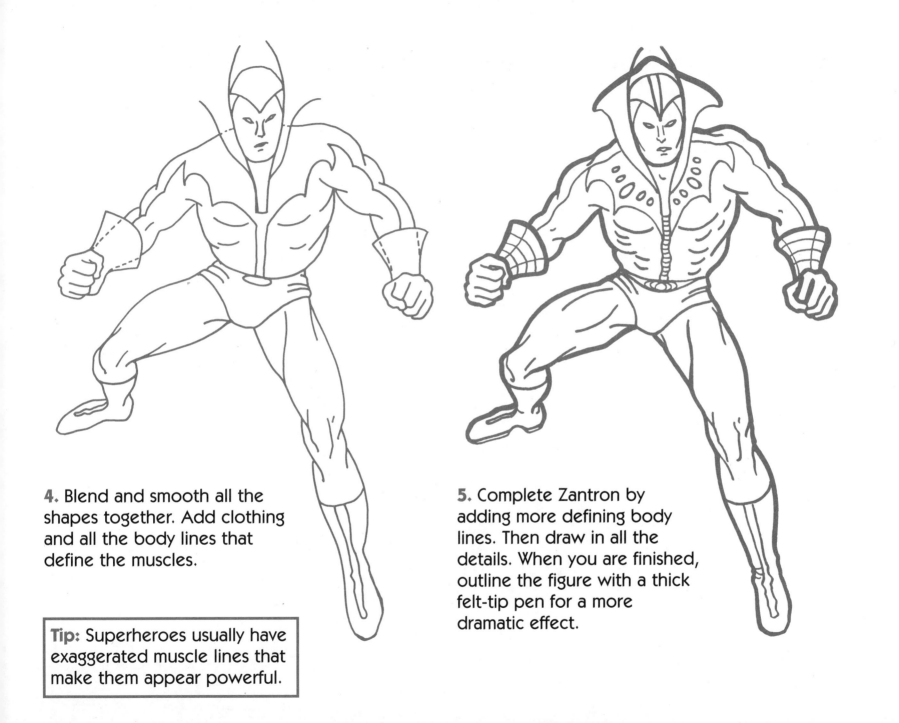

4. Blend and smooth all the shapes together. Add clothing and all the body lines that define the muscles.

Tip: Superheroes usually have exaggerated muscle lines that make them appear powerful.

5. Complete Zantron by adding more defining body lines. Then draw in all the details. When you are finished, outline the figure with a thick felt-tip pen for a more dramatic effect.

Superhero scenery

Here are a couple of examples of the kind of places a superhero might find adventure. Try drawing these as background scenes for some of the characters you draw—or create your own.

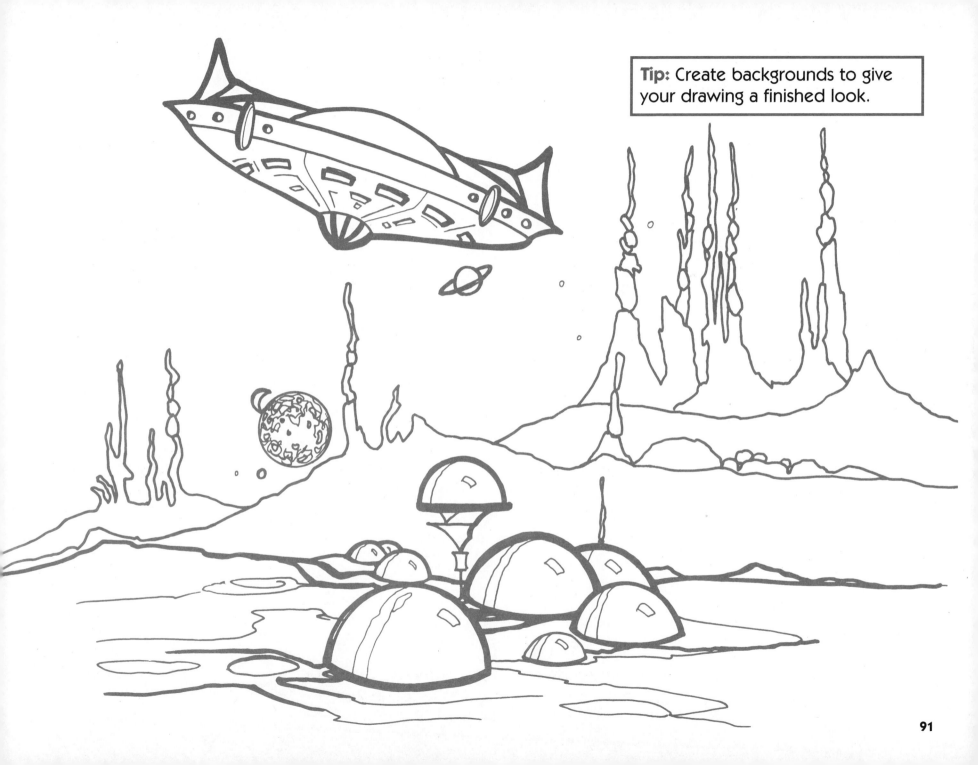

Tip: Create backgrounds to give your drawing a finished look.

INDEX

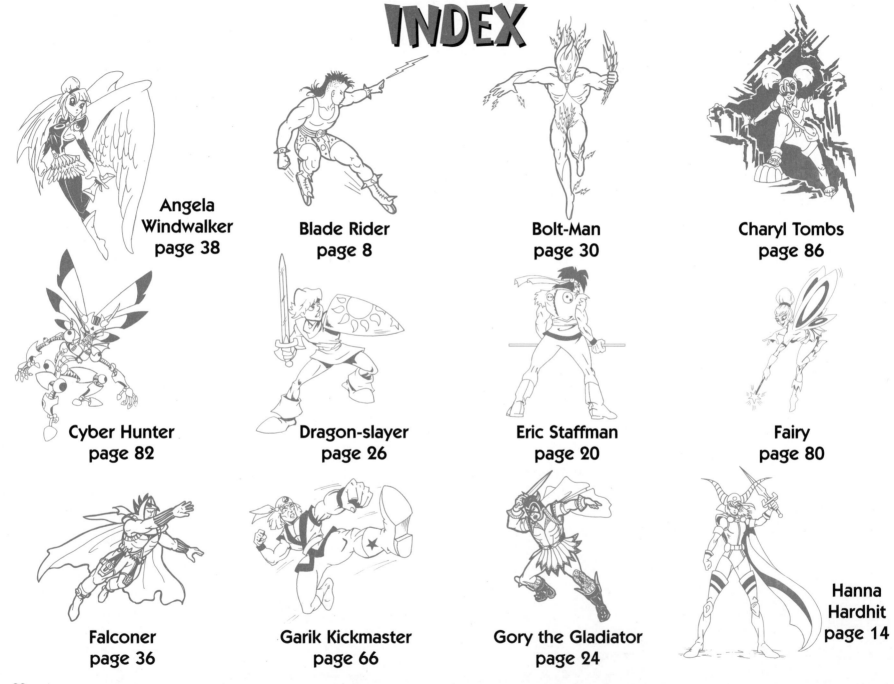

It-Zak Cloud Maker
page 12

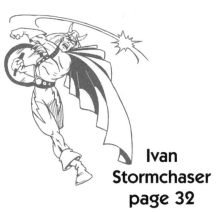

Ivan Stormchaser
page 32

Jantra Adon
page 34

Jason of the Argonauts
page 48

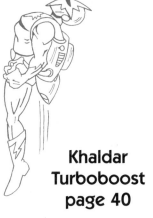

Khaldar Turboboost
page 40

Kid Tempest
page 58

Kit the Courageous
page 18

Kristal Ball
page 16

Lana Laserblast
page 62

Lektra
page 42

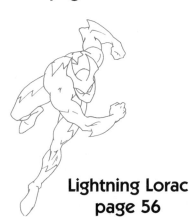

Lightning Lorac
page 56

Luna Leigh
page 70

Marielle
Moonbeam
page 22

Melinda Moderna
page 10

Mighty
Zankon
page 46

Mordecai Magicus
page 74

Nansu Dawn
page 28

Power Puncher
page 50

Princess
Sword
page 54

Quasar-man
page 60

Rahab the Red
page 44

Reflectron
page 64

Robo-man
page 68

She-La Z
page 6

Steelo the Ultimate
page 72

Superhero scenery 1
page 90

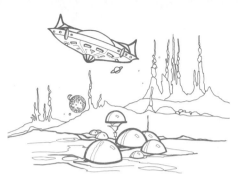

Superhero scenery 2
page 91

Superhero sidekicks
page 81

Thora
page 76

Transflier
page 78

The Vaporizer
page 17

The Vapor Ranger
page 84

Veshti Vanu
page 52

Zantron
page 88

Z. Charger
page 4